Epigraph:

Think not lightly of evil, saying, "It will not come to me."
Drop by drop is the water pot filled.
Likewise, the fool, gathering it little by little,
fills himself with evil.

Think not lightly of good, saying, "It will not come to me."
Drop by drop is the water pot filled.
Likewise, the wise man, gathering it little by little,
fills himself with good.

> The Dhammapada: The Buddha's Path of Wisdom
> #121 and 122
> Translated from the Pali by Acharya Buddharakkhita

"Drop by Drop"
Drip-drop, drop by drop

Let no one think lightly of good deeds
That nothing will come of them.
Even by falling water drops
A water tub fills.
(Drop by drop, fill a water tub. It will surely fill.)

Drop by drop, it fills up.
Bit by bit, enlightenment.
Drop by drop.

> Text and Music by Charles Burdick (2008)

Living As Though There Is a Tomorrow,

Creating the Future by Choice Using Reason, Duty, Love, and Belief:

A Practical Handbook for Moral Growth

By Phyllis Ballata

Order this book online at www.trafford.com/08-0300
or email orders@trafford.com

Most Trafford titles are also available at major online book retailers.

© Copyright 2008 Phyllis L. Ballata.

All rights reserved. No part of this publication may be reproduced, stored in a retrieval system, or transmitted, in any form or by any means, electronic, mechanical, photocopying, recording, or otherwise, without the written prior permission of the author.

Note for Librarians: A cataloguing record for this book is available from Library and Archives Canada at www.collectionscanada.ca/amicus/index-e.html

Printed in Victoria, BC, Canada.

ISBN: 978-1-4251-7290-9

We at Trafford believe that it is the responsibility of us all, as both individuals and corporations, to make choices that are environmentally and socially sound. You, in turn, are supporting this responsible conduct each time you purchase a Trafford book, or make use of our publishing services. To find out how you are helping, please visit www.trafford.com/responsiblepublishing.html

Our mission is to efficiently provide the world's finest, most comprehensive book publishing service, enabling every author to experience success. To find out how to publish your book, your way, and have it available worldwide, visit us online at www.trafford.com/10510

 www.trafford.com

North America & international
toll-free: 1 888 232 4444 (USA & Canada)
phone: 250 383 6864 ♦ fax: 250 383 6804 ♦ email: info@trafford.com

The United Kingdom & Europe
phone: +44 (0)1865 487 395 ♦ local rate: 0845 230 9601
facsimile: +44 (0)1865 481 507 ♦ email: info.uk@trafford.com

10 9 8 7 6 5 4 3 2

Dedication

To my family, friends, and students
who have given me an opportunity and a reason to think
and to the Oxford Round Table
that gave me an opportunity and a reason to act

In *Living as Though There Is a Tomorrow, Creating the Future by Choice Using Reason, Duty, Love, and Belief* some of the pieces of my lifetime of reading and thinking, being and doing have come together to form this meditation on the importance and meaning of choosing life over death, choosing moral Growth over moral Decay, in the practical, "real" world. These fragments of my life are a unique collection. But my wish is that you will add some of these pieces to your own reason, sense of duty, love of life, and deepest beliefs to create energy for your personal life to Grow. Together we can create a positive future by choice.

Living as Though There Is a Tomorrow,

Creating the Future by Choice
Using Reason, Duty, Love, and Belief:

A Practical Handbook for Moral Growth

By Phyllis Ballata

Contents

<u>Finding Direction</u>

1.0.0 Prologue

2.0.0 The Model of Moral Growth and Moral Decay

2.1.0 Ethics—Definitions, Characteristics, and Principles

2.1.1 *Thought Experiment: Your Group Dynamics*

2.2.0 The Importance of Choice

2.2.1 *Thought Experiment: Characteristics of Moral Growth and Decay Then and Now*

2.3.0 The Advantages of Decay and the Problems of Choice

2.3.1 Moral Decay is Useful

2.3.2 *Thought Experiment: What and Who is "Better"?*

2.3.3 Moral Decay is Rational

2.3.4 Opposition to Moral Decay is Dangerous

2.3.5 Contagious Spread of Growth and Decay

2.4.0 Factors of Choice for Individuals

2.4.1	Psychological Experiment on Authority and Violence
2.4.2	*Thought Experiment: Responsibilities of Leaders and Followers*
2.4.3	Awareness
2.4.4	*Thought Experiment: Awareness of Causes and Effects*
2.5.0	Freedom to Choose
2.5.1	Principles of Freedom and Awareness
2.5.2	*Thought Experiment: Means and Ends*
2.6.0	Acting for the Common Good
2.6.1	Life Cycle Analysis
2.6.2	*Thought Experiment: Analysis of Purchases*

Paths and Choices

3.0.0	Paths in the Family
3.1.0	Contagion and Needs for Growth and Decay
3.1.1	*Thought Experiment: Influences*
3.2.0	Parenting
3.2.1	*Thought Experiment: Parenting Styles*
3.2.2	*Thought Experiment: Family Growth*
3.2.3	*Thought Experiment: Getting Out of the Self*
3.2.4	Rachel Carson's "Sense of Wonder"

4.0.0	Paths in Education
4.1.0	Public Education
4.1.1	Teaching Styles
4.1.2	*Thought Experiment: Teacher-Student Cause-Effect*
4.1.3	*Thought Experiment: Boss-Worker, Mentor-Learner, President-Citizen Cause-Effect*
4.1.4	*Thought Experiment: Goals for Teaching*
4.1.5	Analysis: Why do these help Growth? How can they be made real?

4.1.6	*Thought Experiment: Doing More than One Thing with Multiple Goals*
5.0.0	Paths in Local Community
5.1.0	Citizenship
5.1.1	*Thought Experiment: Local Opportunities for Growth*
5.1.2	*Thought Experiment: Local Responsibilities*
5.2.0	Leadership
5.2.1	Qualities in a Leader
6.0.0	Paths in State/Province/Region
6.1.0	Education
6.1.1	*Thought Experiment: Defining Public Education*
6.1.2	Education to Encourage Growth
6.1.3	Using Resources Effectively
6.2.0	Justice and Equity in Democracy
6.2.1	*Thought Experiment: Defining Justice*
6.2.2	Characteristics of Justice
6.2.3	*Thought Experiment: Justice in Action*
6.3.0	Prisons
6.3.1	*Thought Experiment: Growth in Prison?*
6.3.2	Purpose of Prison
6.3.3	Suggestions for Change
6.3.4	*Thought Experiment: What Would You Need?*
6.4.0	Reversing or Preventing Decay
6.4.1	Lessons from the Stanford Prison Experiment: Dangers of Unlimited Power
6.4.2	Requirements for Reversing Opportunities for Decay
6.4.3	*Thought Experiment: Dangers of the Use of Power*
6.5.0	Right Use of Power in Everyday Life
6.5.1	Need for Oversight
6.5.2	Personal Oversight

6.5.3	Transparency
6.5.4	*Thought Experiment: Methods of Oversight*
6.6.0	Helping the Neighbor and the Stranger
6.6.1	*Thought Experiment: Who Would Help?*
6.6.2	Helping the Whole Person
6.7.0	Taxes as Resources for the Common Good
6.7.1	*Thought Experiment: Taxes as Rewards and Punishments*
6.7.2	The Purposes and Effects of a Tax System
6.7.3	Consequences of a Tax System
6.7.4	*Thought Experiment: Focusing the System*
7.0.0	Paths for the Nation
7.1.0	Swarm Theory
7.1.1	Being Collectively Smart
7.2.0	Realism and Growth or Decay
7.2.1	Growth and Decay in Stories/Literature
7.2.2	*Thought Experiment: Core Principles*
7.2.3	"Authoritative" National Policy
7.2.4	*Thought Experiment: National Growth and Decay*
7.3.0	Economics
7.3.1	Economic Systems
7.3.2	*Thought Experiment: Priorities*
7.4.0	Public Policy and the Common Good
7.4.1	*Thought Experiment: National Government Representing All Citizens*
7.5.0	Military
7.5.1	War
7.5.2	The Enemy
7.5.3	Inhumanity
7.5.4	American Military
7.5.5	Decay as Failure of Imagination
7.5.6	*Thought Experiment: Citizen Questions in an External Crisis*

7.5.7	*Thought Experiment: Citizen Questions in an Internal Crisis*
7.6.0	What Should We Export?
7.6.1	Defining Freedom, Choice, and Success
7.6.2	*Thought Experiment: Tensions in Values*
7.7.0	Foreign Policy
7.7.1	Policies Leading to Decay
7.7.2	*Thought Experiment: Imagining Foreign Aid*
7.7.3	*Thought Experiment: Designing a Foreign Aid System*
7.7.4	Foreign Aid for Growth
7.7.5	Suggestions for Foreign Aid
7.7.6	Threats to Growth
7.7.7	Dangers of Decay in Foreign Aid
7.7.8	Suggestions for Avoiding Decay in Foreign Aid
7.7.9	*Thought Experiment: Walking in Another's Shoes*
8.0.0	Social Choices and Consequences
8.1.0	Defining Consequences
8.1.1	Rational and Practical vs. Irrational and Impractical
8.1.2	Creating Our World by Choice
8.1.3	Actual Choices
8.1.4	Choosing our Relationship to Nature
8.1.5	Questioning for the Common Good
8.1.6	*Thought Experiment: What is the Public Good?*
8.1.7	Choosing a Path toward Moral Growth
8.2.0	Contagion and Inoculation
8.2.1	Inoculation against Growth is Easy
8.2.2	Disabling Growth Piece by Piece
8.2.3	Inoculation against Decay is Planted by Example
8.3.0	Innocence and Experience
8.3.1	Positive and Negative Innocence

A Practical Handbook for Moral Growth   10

8.3.2   Negative and Positive Experience

8.3.3   Growth as Positive Experience

8.3.4   Growth as a Whole Unit

8.3.5   Growth as a Source of Ethics

<u>Future Thoughts</u>

9.0.0   Discovery of Choices and Consequences

9.1.0   *Thought Experiment, continuing into the future: Personal Discoveries*

9.2.0   *Thought Experiment, continuing into the future: Freedom and Awareness in Creating a Self-Governing Society*

9.3.0   *Thought Experiment, continuing into the future: Freedom and Awareness in Creating a Self-Governing Individual*

10.0.0   Wisdom from Many Places, Traditions, and Voices: A Bibliography of some ideas influencing the text

11.0.0   Using this Handbook

12.0.0   Appendix

12.1.0   Speech—"Growth: A Foundation for Sustainable Environmental and Humanitarian Ethics" by Phyllis Ballata. Oxford Round Table, 2007. St. Anne's College, Oxford University, Oxford, England

Living As Though There Is a Tomorrow,

Creating the Future by Choice
Using Reason, Duty, Love, and Belief:

A Practical Handbook for Moral Growth

"No important change in ethics was ever accomplished
without an internal change in our
intellectual emphasis, loyalties, affections, and convictions."
"The Land Ethic" by Aldo Leopold

FINDING DIRECTION

1.0.0   Prologue

We each create the future everyday by making concrete, practical choices large and small, for better or worse at every level of life. We choose at home, at work, and in the voting booth. We choose as individuals, as communities, as a nation, even as a world. As the saying goes, even choosing not to choose is choosing. From these choices come specific consequences. Our choices are better or worse because there is such a thing as right and wrong, moral Growth and moral Decay. The conflict between them influences our lives, every other living thing, and the earth itself in all sorts of ways.

Each choice can be imagined as an individual dot along the age axis of our lives. Yet as our choices accumulate over time, they create patterns of behaviors and actions, gradually clustering toward Growth or moving toward Decay. We all have "outliers" that we might say are uncharacteristic of us, in either direction. We also have clusters of choices resulting from the specific influences of others, from our personal experiences, and from moments of crisis or reflection.

The consequences of our choices as individuals or groups are complex and not always easy to analyze. One might think that people would, naturally, choose moral Growth because everyone is basically good. Or at least they would pretend to be good if they noticed someone else watching. In fact, it probably depends on who is watching. The most we could say is that everyone has the potential for moral Growth.

On the other hand, moral Decay is certainly very effective for short term accumulation of power and wealth by individuals, groups, and governments. Immediate power and wealth or looking out for number one is a "rational choice," as Jared Diamond illustrates in Collapse: How Societies Choose to Fail or Succeed, even though it may eventually lead to disaster. We may condemn Machiavelli's advice in The Prince, but if the goal is personal power, then his advice—even though it leads ultimately to Decay—is rational for achieving the goal.

The critical issues are "What is my goal?" "What am I doing?" "Why am I doing this?" "Is what I am choosing actually leading to the goal?" and "Is the goal right, good, important, or just for whom?"

In our work, in our organizations, in our businesses, and in our governments, we need to ask the same questions: "What is our goal?" "What are we doing?" "Why are we doing this?" "Is what we are choosing actually leading to the goal?" and "Is the goal right, good, important, or just—for whom?"

Asking these questions helps us to live as though there is a tomorrow. When we spend some time dissecting our choices and their consequences, we can discover what we really want in our personal lives and in the groups that we belong to. What are the actual possibilities for behavior and action? What are the actual consequences—short term and long term? These discoveries will be useful or disconcerting or both.

Living As Though There Is a Tomorrow, Creating the Future Using Reason, Duty, Love, and Belief argues for making consciously ethical choices.

Two basic points are in question.

First, is there such a thing as right and wrong, moral Growth and moral Decay? Many would say no. They would argue that everything humans think and do is relative: relative to culture and social influences, relative to religious or philosophical teaching, relative to time and place. This leads to the idea that as long as an individual sincerely believes something, then who are we to disagree? Unfortunately, this also leaves us with nothing to say to the person who sincerely believes he should blow himself up in the market or to the person who sincerely believes that genocide is necessary or to the person who sincerely believes his right to wealth or power is the only pertinent concern. It also leads to the idea, for example, that the law trumps honesty and justice. If I follow the letter of the law, that is enough—I don't need to also be personally honest and just. It's all relative. I believe that as humans we need to have something to say about these issues. As a result this Practical Handbook is based on the belief that there is such a thing as right and wrong, better or worse— even that moral Growth and moral Decay are built into the fact of humanness, and we need to discover, examine, and face them.

The second question is whether we are willing or even able to discuss morality in the public sphere. All over the world this topic seems to be reserved for our personal and private languages of religion or politics or culture. Can we find words to use that transcend our differences and focus instead on our common humanity? The weight of our sheer numbers and our immense technological power is bearing down on us. Can we find the will and the words while we still have time to create our future by positive choices?

I believe that moral Growth is better than moral Decay and will try to prove that. But anyone might easily discover that his or her real goal is what I call Decay. Decay provides immediate personal power and wealth that could be more important than anyone or anything else. For thousands of years great thinkers have warned humanity against choosing a path toward Decay. Even so, we still continue to choose Decay for the same reasons as humans have always chosen it—status, money, or power.

The Thought Experiments in the Practical Handbook lead to personal applications and immediate interactions with the ideas and problems we all face everyday. Humans are uniquely capable of "thought experiments" because our brains go beyond solving an immediate problem (as other animal brains can do) to imagining the problem and simulating our possible behaviors to test the consequences. Philosopher Karl Popper says that this process allows "our hypothesis to die in our stead." While this probably happens both consciously and unconsciously, in the Practical Handbook's Thought Experiments we can make it conscious.

One sign of human intelligence is our ability to make these internal models for testing our assumptions and actions. This leads to thinking, believing, wishing, and understanding as well as doing. From this we have the potential to see and imagine the future. We can see what we want to aim for and plan how to get there. Still the question remains: what do we want to aim for?

We all make ethical choices based on our conscious or unconscious goals, so Living as Though There is a Tomorrow is designed to help us sort out the long term consequences. I hope we do choose to live our lives as though there is a tomorrow. I hope we do learn how to combine our reason, our sense of duty, our love, and our beliefs to make ethical choices.

If we want to grow personally or in our families, communities, or political systems, we have a chance of getting there, step by step. It is easy to see this process as a waste of time, a "serious" exercise that is no fun. Some might argue that we should live our lives by instinct, governed by "whatever" because it is just too much bother to see, think, analyze, and choose. We are too busy running to and fro, gathering and piling up our possessions, and entertaining ourselves to be bothered with long-term thinking. What have we got to lose but our souls and our future? But, awareness of the choices we make and the actions we take can be the first step into a future that we are consciously creating everyday—for good, rather than for ill.

There are no prescriptive actions here—each of us decides what to do moment by moment. First come thinking and wishing (as Aldo Leopold says), then aiming (as Henry David Thoreau says); then come specific actions and their natural consequences. Let's talk about our long term goals and the consequences of our thinking and wishing in order to find the direction to go. Let's see where the pathways lead, discover what our choices are, and then use our individual freedom to decide on our course of action.

2.0.0   The Model of Moral Growth and Moral Decay

In an interconnected world of diversity and complexity, we humans need some *public language*, some *public vocabulary* in order to discuss our mutual needs and concerns. Living as Though There Is a

Tomorrow, Creating the Future by Choice Using Reason, Duty, Love, and Belief provides a suggestion for that public language. If our language about ethics is only understood in our individual private worlds, our private religions, or our private political circles, then we cannot discuss deep issues together.

In addition the model of moral Growth and moral Decay is an outgrowth of thousands of years of human philosophy. This is not a new or unique vocabulary. The difference is that now humans are so many and so powerful that whatever we choose to do about moral Growth and moral Decay affects every life on earth and the very earth itself.

The questions of moral Growth and moral Decay come down to us through the ages as well as through our human sense of inner harmony or inner dissonance. Yet passing on an ethical perspective does not happen by accident. Each generation must choose to pass on these questions as well as a belief in ethical Growth to the next generation. No learning is permanent—all must be deliberately passed on. If we leave this responsibility to advertisers or demagogues, Decay and rot are set free to create a plague of moral infection. When a generation loses focus on the questions that make tomorrow healthy, the people, the entire nation, and the human and natural world suffer.

At the foundational level, this discussion begins building on philosopher Erich Fromm's (1900-1980) observations of human behavior in both ordinary and extraordinary situations, especially as he explains it in _The Heart of Man: Its Genius for Good and Evil_. However, we won't use Fromm's model exactly as he did in his struggle to understand the great evils of Nazism and the Holocaust of World War II. Instead, we will move toward a wider view that encompasses all kinds of decisions, large and small. This version of moral Growth and moral Decay helps us analyze attitudes and behaviors as we see them at all levels of human society, from individuals to communities to nations.

For this purpose we need to avoid getting trapped in theoretical disputes that are unending and impossible to resolve into practical action—because we need practical action. So we will step around the jargon of psychology and psychological theories, even though they would be useful in other circumstances. We also need to step around arguments about particular religious theologies. Although the issues in the Practical Handbook can certainly be related to religion, they do not have to be filtered through any one specific religious perspective. Catholic, Protestant, or Orthodox Christians; Jews or Muslims; Buddhists or Hindus or Taoists; and followers of indigenous beliefs, Greek philosophy, or scientific humanism would be equally able to enter this thought experiment. Instead we will test and analyze our thinking about moral Growth and moral Decay as we face practical, real-world decisions and actions. Let's ask basic questions: What do I think and what should I do? What do we think and what should we do?

The issue includes several parts. First, what are the facts and terms of this conflict between moral Growth and moral Decay—if there is such a thing? Then how should we interpret the meanings of these facts and terms in concrete, specific situations? Finally, what do these facts and interpretations mean to us? If we apply them in our lives, what will our choices be? What will the consequences of those choices be—for us, for our families, for our communities, states, and nations, and for the natural world? Once we have become aware of our choices and their consequences, we can take hold of our freedom to act on this awareness.

Surely it is easier to think in theoretical terms. We could pretend that if we had a choice, we would do X. But, of course, avoiding reality and staying safely inside theory means we don't have to make a choice or use our freedom to act. This protects us from concrete realities. Our ethics are locked inside our heads or hearts. In this pretend world, we can keep our theories safe from the competition, conflicts, and consequences of the specific world all around us. In Areopagitica (1644) John Milton doubts the value of a "fugitive and cloistered virtue," one that has been hidden away from testing and protected from making choices. Rather we must encounter the real choices of life, think for ourselves, and act. *Joys Sorrows*

The integration of head and heart with words and deeds is crucial. We need to be whole—we need to think, feel, and act. Keeping our real selves bottled up inside is painful and dangerous. Both physicians and philosophers have long warned us that the characteristics of Decay lead to physical, mental, emotional, and spiritual illness. But the issue of choosing ethical Growth or Decay is not a theoretical or self-serving question. As individuals and as members of groups, we need to understand our actual behavior and our actual choices more clearly. We need to recognize that both Growth and Decay are entirely real and logical choices. The question is in what direction are our cumulative choices gradually heading? Since moral Growth and moral Decay are contagious, what kinds of atmosphere, tone, or gesture are influencing us how are we influencing others? Will our choices heal or kill?

We also need to resist the temptation to believe that really all people would choose Growth if they just knew the facts. Growth and Decay are at war in us (and have always been at war in us) because they are equally strong, but effective for different reasons and with different results. In fact, Decay is often stronger in the short term and for personal advantage—even though this can be a dangerous advantage for others and for the natural world. There are many "good" reasons to choose Decay. We need to confront them out in the open.

American popular culture includes many Decay-inducing values. We sometimes ignore them because they sneak in under our radar or in disguise, but the rot of these misunderstandings can destroy us gradually. Decay eats away at the foundations of a courageous, independent, loving life. Should we choose the temporary fun that everyone else seems to see and cheer or should we choose a sense of lasting internal joy? Should we choose instant thrills and excitement with a crowd over a mentally and emotionally stimulating and interesting life that would demand individual commitment and effort? Should we take mindless risks without awareness of the long term consequences, or can we face the intrinsic adventures of life with courage and knowledge? Do we believe we deserve comfort and ease without work? Do we want security and safety more than responsibility and freedom? Do we make ourselves the measure of all things, full of self-absorption, self-centeredness, and self-concern rather than noticing and taking into account all the other lives around us?

Detours can take us far off the road of moral Growth. Families and schools too often take away the difficulties of personal responsibility, courage, and effort while substituting the easy way of blaming, cowardice, and laziness. Commercial culture based on greed, fear, and envy leads us into gullies where flash floods of advertising carry us away. Political policies based on anxiety, power, and self-righteousness undermine everything we wish to stand for in the wider world. We are bound up by conformity and uniformity, rather than being aware of the many possibilities of freedom and individuality that are available to us. Even for the poorest among us, as long as there is consciousness there is choice, if only as a single individual in a single moment.

Are we trapped? If we were to choose ethical Growth, how would we deal with our own minds and hearts? With both neighbors and strangers? With the natural world? What policies would we support concerning education, justice, or foreign aid? War and peace? Let's examine the possible choices and their consequences, our responsibilities, and the meaning of freedom.

2.1.0   Ethics—Definitions, Characteristics, and Principles

Examine and analyze this list of the characteristics, causes, and effects of moral Growth and moral Decay in detail. Spending some time thinking about each of these individually and about the pairings in the list will be a great help in understanding the complexity as well as the unity of the model itself.

By adapting Fromm's basic pattern to the discussion at hand, we can arrive at a broader analysis. The basic principles of our model of moral Growth and moral Decay are these:

Characteristics of Moral Growth
- attraction to or love of life and its processes
- love of others that moves out from the self to neighbors, strangers, and nature or all living things (even, as Aldo Leopold would argue, to the land itself, the air, and the waters)
- willingness to risk action based on independence, freedom, responsibility, and personal choice

Characteristics of Moral Decay
- attraction to or love of death, force, violence, mechanism, and power and their processes
- extreme self-love, self-focus, and absolutism
- parasitic dependence, fear, and authoritarianism

Causes and Effects of Growth

love of life
love of others (neighbor, stranger, nature)
mental and moral independence
productive activity and life
economic sufficiency
mental/psychological abundance
reason, objectivity, rational judgment
rational thought, critical thinking
awareness of reality
acceptance of truth as valid for all
orientation to present and future
integrated and united personality
structural and intellectual growth
love for processes of life,
personal feeling and thinking
service to and defense of life
enlarged circle of life
joy and gladness
warm, affectionate human contacts
freedom
courage
inner harmony and strength
stimulating life; interest in life
direct human relations with people as people
justice for all equally
dignified life without fear and anxiety
dignified life for all people
freedom to be active and responsible in society
basic security; realistic expectation of future security
personal and specific experience of life
original, daring, adventurous character
experience of self as individual, separate but open

A Practical Handbook for Moral Growth

Causes and Effects of Decay

love of death

love of self or personal select-group

mental and moral dependence

incompetence, impotence

economic scarcity or pov.

mental/psychological poverty

surrender to passions, total subjectivity

irrational or uncritical thought

unrealistic fanaticism and group narcissism

truth as valid for self and personal group only

orientation to past or to vengeance

extreme dependence on leaders, cult of personality

weakness, anxiety, stagnation

fascination with death and mechanical order

suffering through life, passivity

love of force; willingness to kill without thought

narrow definition of life

addiction to thrills or excitement

despair, cynicism, loss of trust

unquestioning submission

fright, threat

inner dissonance, crippling and emptiness

lack of stimulation; lack of interest in life; boredom

obsession with law and order

injustice; inequality; justice only for self or personal group

fear; anxiety; cultural poverty

others seen as inferior or nonhuman

absolute obedience

constant fear and threats; realistic or imagined fear for future

living through or worship of protector, group, or nation

self as consumed by or consuming others

experience of self as dependent, narcissistic, closed

Causes and Effects of Growth

awareness of self as a complete human

concern for the common good

acceptance of useful tasks and equity

acceptance of the risks of responsibility

awareness and acceptance of the power and responsibility to choose

aware of inner forces or rationalizations

awareness that others expect a loving response

acceptance of the reality of uncertainty and risk

independence, freedom, responsibility

helpfulness

awareness of realistic alternatives and consequences

favorable development

creative imagination

willing to act

willingness to struggle with frustration

fortitude, insight, effort

self-confidence, integrity, courage

acceptance of the burdens of humanness

individual choices in real life

concrete, specific actions from choices

loving, productive, independent

A Practical Handbook for Moral Growth

Causes and Effects of Decay
experience of self as incomplete, empty
good for self and personal group only
exploitation of others
overwhelming concern for personal safety
unawareness or denial of the reality of personal choice
unaware of inner forces or rationalizations
preoccupation with self; others are unreal
filled with anxieties, whether real or unreal
dependence; avoidance of responsibility
helplessness
unrealistic expectations and assumptions
weak or no development
stagnation, regression, lack of creativity
unwilling to act
unwilling to struggle with frustration
weakness, lack of insight, impotence
cowardice
incapable of or above bearing life's burdens
personal moral or ethical paralysis
inability to choose or act
destructive, impotent, dependent

After examining this list in detail, consider how you have seen particular characteristics play out in the world, in behaviors and relationships. Once we do this, choices and actions of all types can become more clear and understandable. We can consider them more thoughtfully and choose more wisely.

<u>All of us sometimes choose or act toward Decay and sometimes toward Growth</u>. We waver back and forth, gradually trending in one direction or the other. To cite a simple example, the first time you consider stopping yourself from dropping a candy

wrapper on the ground, it might be difficult to even notice what you are doing, to say nothing of choosing to put the wrapper in your pocket until you come to a wastebasket. But it gradually becomes a habit. Eventually the very thought of throwing that candy wrapper on the ground is almost impossible to consider. But in a crowd of people who are leaving litter around, it is much easier to do because it suddenly seems normal. Choosing toward Decay gradually makes choosing Decay easier and more natural. On the other hand, choosing toward Growth gradually leads to more Growth. The power of habit is strong, but not invincible. Our attitudes and behaviors are contagious.

2.1.1 *Thought Experiment: Your Group Dynamics*

Consider the dynamics in a group you belong to—your immediate friends, your work, school, or civic organization.

What characteristics of Growth or Decay do you see in the various people who belong to your groups?

How might you act differently in these various groups in order to fit in?

Why would you act or think differently depending on which group you were with?

Are you consciously or unconsciously doing this?

Think of a specific person.

What might his or her reasons be for choosing the actions or characteristics of Growth or Decay?

Do you believe that person is choosing?

Is he or she "controlled" by something or someone external?

Is he or she "controlled" by internal assumptions or beliefs?

What might change how this person acts—for better or worse?

Consider your religious or political group.

Does the group act in a way consistent with what it says?

Does your group say one thing but do another?

Do the rules or expectations of the group apply to all equally?

Is there one rule for "us" and another rule for "them"?
Is there one rule for the leader and another rule for the followers?

It is often easier to analyze others than to analyze ourselves, of course. And seeing the concrete effects of someone else's behavior and choices is easier than imagining how we ourselves might act in a variety of circumstances. It is often hard to foresee and then to choose what to do about the negative consequences of moral Decay or to choose how to strengthen moral Growth. But noticing is the first step.

2.2.0   The Importance of Choice

Could moral Decay be useful? Could moral Growth be a problem?

It is not wise to be too simplistic about something this complex and intensely human. Throughout history humans have observed and responded to the characteristics of Growth and Decay. The dark and the light, the low road and the high road, the powers of evil and good, choosing death or life have been archetypes for as long as human stories have been told. In our age-old stories we have tried to explain ourselves to ourselves.

In the Genesis stories the possibility of Growth or Decay is built into the Garden. The choice is there before any action. The division within humans is part of the beginning of humanity, and there is no procreation until after the "fall." Further, the temptation is to "be like God" knowing good from evil, and thus being capable of choosing good or evil and <u>knowing</u> it.

Sometimes we rationalize that the characteristics of moral Decay are a just a necessary means toward what we hope and expect will be a good result. We have a good reason to choose Decay! We believe that we will not be harmed by our choices (whether we would be King David or Faust or Darth Vader), but accepting Decay as if it were a temporary necessity or a minor detour is the stuff of tragedy. Strangely, in our stories the villain is often more interesting, more exciting than the so-called hero. Even though we know whom we are supposed to cheer for, Milton's Satan is somehow so much more detailed and complex than Milton's God in Paradise Lost. The tragedy makes such a good story—but such a painful life.

Erich Fromm sees a difference between archaic or tribal groups and more enlightened cultures. He defines "enlightened" cultures as the monotheistic religions of Egypt and the descendants of Abraham, the teachings of Moses and the Hebrew Prophets, Buddha, Lao-tse, Confucius, Greek philosophers, Christ and Christian theologians, Mohammed and Islamic commentators, and the European Enlightenment and scientific thinkers. Each of these traditions attempts to go beyond blood lust and tribalism. [Side note: In a related comparison, Thomas Cahill in Sailing the Wine Dark Sea: Why the Greeks Matter discusses this difference. He sees Homer's Iliad as an example of what Fromm would describe as a tribal culture controlled by war and bloodlust, but Homer's Odyssey as a "new" way of seeing that emphasizes the importance of personal emotion, home, and family, what Fromm would define as a more enlightened culture.] These enlightened societies are characterized by recognizable philosophies. In them we find parallel conflicts between the ideal and the real, between Growth and Decay.

Notice how natural it is for us to say that Growth is ideal, but Decay is real?

No tradition escapes the results of human nature because all are expressions of the human condition. Essentially the basic struggles

A Practical Handbook for Moral Growth 28

of life have been and are still between moral Growth and moral Decay. From ancient days to today, humanness is the constant. We wear different clothes, travel in different ways, communicate with different devices, kill each other or love each other in a wide variety of circumstances—yet humans still struggle with these basic choices and actions.

2.2.1 *Thought Experiment:*
Characteristics of Moral Growth and Decay
Then and Now

Go back to the list of the causes and effects of moral Growth and Decay (2.1.0).
Thinking of all the earth's cultures and peoples, past and present, are any of these characteristics only true today?
Were any only true 2000 years ago?
Were any only true 6000 years ago?
Have any of the conflicts been resolved or eliminated?
Do these conflicts still exist?
What do the stories of your culture show you about human nature?

2.3.0   The Advantages of Decay and the Problems of Growth

2.3.1   Moral Decay is Useful

Moral Decay is useful for getting and keeping power and for accumulating wealth. We see the characteristics of moral Decay around us all the time. Advertisers often depend on and play with our fears and greed, our envy and jealousy. We are encouraged to buy deodorant because of fears that we smell bad since human odor is repulsive in our society. We buy houses, clothes, or cars based on envy or irrational imagination. Will we really drive that utility vehicle to the road-less mountain top as the advertisement shows? Would we even want to? Would we be arrested if we got to the top? Do we need

3000 or 5000 or more square feet of shelter space for two or three people—even though we know that an entire African village could live in our one house or that a typical Chinese farm would fit on our lawn? Do we really "deserve" expensive hair color or are we just afraid that if we don't have the right kind our friends will think less of us somehow? Do we run cleaner, purer water into our toilets than most of the world has to drink and then flush it away because of habit, thoughtlessness, pride? Is our suggestibility more extreme than anyone else's?

Actually, no. Westerners are simply rich. Throughout history it has always been the prerogative of the rich to waste. That is how humans have shown they are rich. The Chinese Emperor did not have to burn his beautiful silk garments sewn and embroidered by multitudes of women—but he could afford to. It contributed to his cult of personality, it made others less important and less valuable than he, it kept others dependent, and it enlarged his vanity and mystique. Did kings and queens need half a dozen palaces with servants and courtiers standing at the ready in case anyone came by? Did robber barons need to build extravagant mansions? Were the pyramids necessary? What was the purpose of gladiators and exotic animals in Rome? What is the reason for a fast, expensive car? Eskimos need fur coats, but do New Yorkers? Does it matter how many jewels are on the crown or whether the headman of the village has a fancier chair than anyone else? Yes, apparently these things do count and they do matter. But why? What is it about humans that make these actions or things valuable?

Certainly humans have always loved beauty, but we have loved excess more. Excess shows we are powerful and wealthy in some way, even if our version of excess is way too many branded t-shirts or a room full of cheaply-made pseudo-French provincial furniture or too many nights of partying or "hooking up" at the slightest attraction.

Excess shows that we are somehow above or better than others around us.

Caring or being concerned for others has often been judged as a weakness. Actually most of the characteristics of moral Growth have been considered signs of weakness in many cultures, times, and places.

This conflict within our nature creates an inner dissonance, so we solve it by accepting love and care within our small group. We allow duty and patriotism for the sake of the country, provided we can still indulge in injustice or violence or passion against the Enemy or through proxies in the military or the government. We desire "shock and awe" to reassure ourselves that we are in the most powerful group. We allow for love of god as long as it is our god and as long as we can still have power and privilege in the synagogue or the church or the mosque. How we express that power is different, but it struggles to come out. Do I have more books, more elaborate liturgical robes, or more followers than my rivals? Do I have softer bread or harder bread, a softer bed or a harder bed, longer hair or no hair—the contests are different depending on what we see as valuable, but the impetus is the same.

Humans admire those who are "better.". We envy them, are jealous of them, want to copy their behavior and belongings. We want to belong in their group, to fit in with their crowd, to follow their lead. We love to read about the excesses of celebrities, to identify with them fills up our own emptiness, puts interest into our seemingly uninteresting lives, gives us thrills. And also, of course, love and admiration from far away are easier than the reality of loving and admiring within our own homes and lives. Politeness to the stranger or even the neighbor is often easier than kindness in the family.

"Better" is a very real concept, but defining "better" is difficult.

2.3.2 *Thought Experiment: Who and What is "Better"?*

Stop a minute—who would you say is "better" than you are?

Think about this for real, not based on what you think you are supposed to say—why is that person "better"?

Are you "better" than someone?

What are the reasons you might be better?

What are the reasons someone else is better than you are?

2.3.3 Moral Decay is Rational

Perhaps our definitions of "better" can show us what we admire and wish for. Perhaps they can help us recognize our unconscious goals. Is our goal power and privilege? Do we consciously or unconsciously expect obedience and service from others? Is the right to make demands, give orders, or command attention a sign of being "better"? Perhaps what we admire is actually Decay. Theologians and philosophers often argue against admiring moral Decay and recommend admiring moral Growth instead: love, joy, peace, patience, kindness, goodness, faithfulness, gentleness, self control, justice, humility, courage, moderation, wisdom, generosity, good temper, truthfulness, friendliness, modesty.

However, Decay is often "rational." Doesn't it make sense to get as much as I can while I have the chance? As Lynn White argues in "The Tragedy of the Commons," it is entirely logical that my two cows should eat twice what my neighbor's one cow eats as long as the grass is still available in our common field. Why not take that advantage if I can? If I own an oil well shouldn't I pump it out as fast as I can to get the most, the fastest, and before my neighbor drills into the same pool of oil? Why not cut down my forest or catch as many fish as possible in order to ensure a profit this quarter? Shouldn't I pay the least amount possible for milk or for your labor? If I can avoid the expense of putting a safety guard on my milling machine, shouldn't I? What do I gain from sharing? What good is the "common good" to me personally? Shouldn't I take advantage of you before you get a chance to take advantage of me? Look out for Number One—because no one else will.

2.3.4   Opposition to Moral Decay is Dangerous

Clearly moral Decay feeds on itself. It is self perpetuating. To escape from moral Decay requires great effort and struggle with the frustrations that are bound to come. It requires prophets and teachers who will lead in another direction. Teaching others to think, to love, to dream, to question, to rebel, and to care for the poor, for the earth, or for justice is to draw attention to the weaknesses of Decay. But Decay is still powerful, and opposition to it is dangerous. Drinking hemlock, or being crucified, or thrown into a pit, or burned at the stake, or hung, or imprisoned, or assassinated, or beaten, or raped, or beheaded might be likely. The stronger the threat to those deep in Decay, the more powerful is their response. Decay spreads through societies because it is contagious.

2.3.5   Contagious Spread of Growth and Decay

Growth can also spread through societies because it too is contagious.

Consider Erich Fromm's discussion of this contagion from The Heart of Man: "The most important condition for the development of the love of life in the child is for him to be with people who love life. Love of life is just as contagious as love of death. It communicates itself without words, explanations, and certainly without any preaching that one ought to love life. It is expressed in gestures more than in ideas, in the tone of voice more than in words.

It can be observed in the whole atmosphere of a person or group, rather than in the explicit principles and rules according to which they organize their lives. Among the specific conditions necessary for the development of biophilia [love of life] I shall mention the following: warm, affectionate contact with others during infancy; freedom, and absence of threats; teaching—by example rather than by preaching— of the principles conducive to inner harmony and strength; guidance in the 'art of living'; stimulating influence of and response to others; a way of life that is genuinely interesting. The very opposite of these conditions furthers the development of necrophilia [love of death]: growing up among death-loving people; lack of stimulation; fright; conditions which make life routinized and uninteresting; mechanical order instead of one determined by direct and human relations among people."

2.4.0 Factors of Choice for Individuals

Sometimes it is hard to see what the choice is. Sometimes it is hard to see that there used to be a choice, but the time for choosing has passed us by. And sometimes we believe that we have no choice and are trapped.

2.4.1 Psychological Experiment on Authority and Violence

Stanley Milgram's famous psychology experiment from the 1960s asked "experimental subjects" to shock people who appeared to be "doing the wrong thing." These people were actually actors and were not really being shocked, but they were good at pretending to be in pain. This was a telling experiment for a couple of reasons. One, of course, was that the subjects were convinced by "authorities" to obey orders with increasing and obviously painful results for other people whom they did not even know. Apparently once they had started

A Practical Handbook for Moral Growth
34

down this path, the subjects just could not or did not want to refuse to obey. "Authorities" (who were actually conducting the experiment) told them their action was required. The subjects needed to shock these strangers for the success of the project or for the strangers' own good. Maybe some secretly wanted to hurt others, and the authorities gave them the chance to do this for a "good" reason. Perhaps, as long as the authorities told them it was the right thing to do, even convincing them that it was for the best, some were not able to find the line in their personal conscience that they would not cross.

But, secondly, and just as important, the subjects themselves were traumatized by their own actions. They were traumatized even when they knew that the victims were actors—maybe especially when they knew the victims were actors. They knew then that they were capable of deliberately harming others who had done them no harm. They were ashamed and filled with guilt. Clearly the subjects did not realize how they would feel afterwards. The designers of the experiment also did not understand how traumatic the results would be for the unfortunate subjects. In fact, the results were so traumatic that this type of experiment was forbidden as unethical in the early 1970s.

What does this show? Clearly one of things we see is moral Decay and Growth in conflict. Surely we do not want to ignore how difficult it is to say no. Saying no is incredibly difficult when it appears that everyone else is on the other side of an issue. And even harder if the "authorities" are on the other side. Yet . . . the subjects did what they knew was wrong because those in power told them to or perhaps gave them an excuse—but they still knew it was wrong and their consciences would not allow them to ignore this. This is no small lesson. What is the responsibility of those in authority, of the leaders? What is the responsibility of the followers?

2.4.2 *Thought Experiment:*
Responsibilities of Leaders and Followers

When are you in a position of leadership in family, work, social, civic, religious, or political groups?

What is your responsibility to your "followers," of any age or position?

Does your responsibility to other leaders override your responsibility to your "followers"?

When are you in the position of a follower?

What is your responsibility to the leader?

Why does a responsibility exist?

What is your responsibility to your fellow followers?

In what situation does your responsibility to yourself take precedence?

How could you recognize when this happens?

2.4.3 Awareness

Fromm argues that the essential requirement of choice is awareness. In Milgram's psychology experiment, were the subjects aware that they could choose not to participate or that they could stop? What did they think they were doing? If they thought the experiment was worthwhile, did they think that their actions were an appropriate means to getting a good result? Were they coerced by some external or internal force or personal wish? Once they started, did they feel that they must go on, that they had no choice? Being aware of the possibility of various choices is certainly not sufficient if the subject of the experiment doesn't have the personal will to act. However, the subject's actions may cause him or her to suffer from "failure" or rejection or from the sarcasm or disappointment of the "authorities."

According to Fromm, awareness includes many steps:
1. Awareness of what final result is better or worse, right or wrong— as well as which means to the end are better or worse;

A Practical Handbook for Moral Growth   36

2. Awareness of which concrete action in the specific situation is an appropriate means to the desired end;

3. Awareness of the forces behind one's apparent wishes, including unconscious desires;

4. Awareness of the real possible choices;

5. Awareness of the consequences of each choice;

6. Awareness of the fact that awareness is not effective without the will to act and willingness to suffer the frustration of effort.

How does one learn these things?

2.4.4   *Thought Experiment: Awareness of Causes and Effects*

Think of an ordinary family, school, or work situation when you had to make a specific choice that affected someone else or several others.

How did you decide whether what you did was right or wrong?

Were there authorities in the background who recommended or required certain actions?

Did the result that you wanted justify any means?

In that specific situation, were you aware of a line that you would not cross?

Were some choices that you might have considered just not possible for you?

Were the consequences what you expected?

Did you recognize what the consequences would be in advance?

Did you have to "suffer" for your choice in some way?

2.5.0   Freedom to Choose

Philosophers often argue about freedom. Are we really free? Or are we determined or controlled by our genes, our social situations, our finances, our educations, or our ancestors so that there is no such thing as freedom? This may be an interesting theoretical discussion, but all of us live in the physical and practical world everyday. We face real choices large and small that will inevitably have tangible consequences. Living our lives based on a mindset of helplessness and hopelessness, caught in a web over which we have no influence, is a waste of our short time on this earth.

We <u>have</u> to live as though we have choices. We have to live as though our thoughts and actions matter. We have to live as though there is a tomorrow where our choices will have consequences. Otherwise we are doomed to Decay.

The practical reality is that we do have the freedom to choose, up to a point. The questions are deceptively simple. First, when are we free to actually choose? When is it not yet too late? Second, can we recognize when it is almost too late, but there is still a chance to change course? To do this it is necessary to be awake to the real possibilities. We need to be aware of when the moment of choice comes, when the road is forking. Wishing that things were different or if only we could do X or Y is not productive. Here we need to face reality. We need all of the awareness, insight, and effort we can muster on our own behalf. If we are trying to help others see their choices, how can we encourage their awareness, insight, and effort? In whatever situation we find ourselves, how can we lay out the actual alternatives and probable consequences so that choices can be made consciously and purposely? How can we make choices that we know will be difficult while at the same time understanding that the difficulties are worth the effort and struggle to come?

2.5.1   Principles of Freedom and Awareness

Principles of Freedom and Awareness:
- some choices and actions are indeed better and worse
- some results are better or worse
- some actions are appropriate means to get to the result we want and some are not

A Practical Handbook for Moral Growth   38

- knowing what unconscious desires are influencing us is helpful
- understanding the real consequences of our choices is helpful
- having the will to act and to make a serious effort is necessary
- sometimes we go beyond the possibility of choice and lose the freedom to choose

Let's examine an ordinary example from real life:

If a student decides that doing well in a class is a good or necessary result, then what actions would follow? Is cheating on the first test an appropriate concrete action? The results may be satisfactory if the student is not caught by the teacher or turned in or ostracized by other students. The conscious desire may be to succeed for the moment without doing any work. This might seem to be the easiest way. Perhaps unconsciously the student fears he or she is actually incapable of success. Perhaps he or she has never succeeded before without cheating. Maybe the student feels pressures from family or friends and is afraid of wasting their money or letting them down.

However, the student may unwittingly go beyond the possibility of making another choice because suddenly he or she does not have the necessary skills or knowledge to succeed at the next level. The consequence may be that what seemed easy at first actually turns out to be much harder. Then, the student must choose to go back and spend the extra time to learn the first skills or information plus the new material, frustrating though that may be, or risk failure on the next test. At the time of the third test, the student is now so far behind that success within the timeframe of the course is no longer possible. The possibility of real choice is gone, at least for this course at this time.

Accepting that success in the class is a good goal, where were the turning points? Choosing a different means to the end, a different concrete action, would probably have been wiser in the long run. Unfortunately, studying and practicing rather than cheating are not easy. If the student tries to succeed by his or her own effort, a lower grade may be the result. Complaints may come from family or friends because the results are not as good as they expected or because the choice of study and practice requires effort that takes time away from competing interests. In this case the student has to have the will to continue to study and practice, and even to suffer frustration if necessary, because that choice of action will lead to greater skill on the next test, greater chance of success on the third test, and the possibility of final success in reaching the good goal.

How many times have we all watched as a public figure or maybe a friend disintegrates because the apparently good goal "requires" a small lie? Then the small lie leads to a more complicated set of lies to hide it. Then the fabrication grows into unmanageable proportions until the whole house of cards collapses. The moral of the story, as we are often reminded, is that it's not the first bad deed, but rather the cover-up that blows the house down. Going beyond the possibility of choice often catches us unaware so that we are beyond the line before we stop to think of it.

2.5.2 *Thought Experiment: Means and Ends*

Think of an immediate or small goal.
Why do you consider this a good goal?
How is it worthwhile or important?
What concrete action is appropriate to take toward achieving this goal?
Why do you think you might have chosen this action?
Can you really take this action?
Is it an actual, possible choice in the real world you live in?
What will the consequences be if you take this action?
What will the consequences be if you achieve the goal?
Are you willing to act, not just imagine?

A Practical Handbook for Moral Growth   40

Are you willing to commit to effort even though it may not be easy or you may not even be successful?

2.6.0   Acting for the Common Good

Many reject the existence or value of the "common good" because they believe that the essence of life is competition. They see winning as much as possible for themselves as the goal. In large part, whether this tends toward moral Growth or Decay depends on how they treat others. Are others just means to use on the way to personal advantage? Are rules just for others to follow? Is reciprocity something that others owe? Is responsibility required of others but never given in return? Are rights more important than duties? If these are true, then this self-centered, self-focused form of "independence" is leading to moral Decay that uses others as objects, demands service but never serves, and exhibits total self-concern.

Others reject the common good because historically it has been corrupted into sacrifice for the Reich or for a nationalistic cause or for a charismatic leader. But the common good is not focused on the power of a small group. It is not created by a demagogue to encourage violence or to excuse authoritarianism. The characteristics of Growth must be true for the common good to exist.

The characteristics of Growth (2.1.0) involve considering what is good for life, for independence, and for freedom—for me, but also for my neighbors, for strangers, for the natural world. When we consider all of these together, this leads us to discover the common good. This questioning involves the logic of cause and effect, backward and forward in time. What result do we want in the long run? What might lead there? If we choose a specific action, what will be the result?

Learning this kind of thinking is based first on the examples of the people that children observe, and then on a parent or teacher or mentor who explains how the process of thinking works and empowers the child's own decision making process. As we grow, we gradually learn to foresee what the consequences might be. We gradually learn to choose our means as well as the ends we aim for.

The common good requires us to apply these choices not only to ourselves, but also to others, neighbors and strangers, and even all living things. In order to make our powers of reasoning, logic, and understanding strong, the causes and effects need to be examined. We need to see that the consequences of our choices extend far beyond ourselves. If we love life itself and love living things beyond ourselves, then we are required to examine both the means and the ends.

It is impossible to do only one thing—in the human world or the natural world. In all of life, all things are connected in webs of relationships.

2.6.1   Life Cycle Analysis for Choosing How to Spend Money

This series of questions leads outward from the self to the rest of the world in many directions. It asks us to understand what our choices are doing to and for others—neighbors, strangers, nature— and then to choose or act on that understanding.

Product Analysis:
What raw materials go into this product?
- How is each of the raw materials made, mined, or grown?
- Where do the materials come from?
- What effects do the manufacturing, discovery, mining, or growing have on the people and land where the materials come from?

A Practical Handbook for Moral Growth

- What kind of waste and/or pollution results from these processes?
- What social and economic effects are produced from these processes? Who gains or loses?

How is the product produced?

- What are the processes involved in its production?
- What effect does its production have on the people who make it, the neighbors of the manufacturing plant, or the land where it is made?
- What local social or economic effects come from these processes?
- Is the company's production environmentally and socially responsible and ethical?
- How and how far is the product shipped?

What waste is created by the product?

- Is the packaging reasonable, excessive, or hazardous?
- What does the packaging itself do to or for the land or the people during its life?
- Can the product or the packaging be reused or recycled? Will it be?
- What will happen to the product when its original usefulness is over?

Who sells the product?

- Who owns the retail establishment, whether in place or "virtual," and where do the profits go?
- Is the retailer environmentally and socially responsible, especially within the local community? Is there a local community?

- Does the retailer make the local community or the larger community a better place to live: more beautiful, more just, more equitable?

[The Nest, White Bear Lake, MN]

2.6.2 *Thought Experiment: Analysis of Purchases*

First, choose your last purchase—a shirt, an apple, a cup of coffee, a DVD—and answer all the questions above for its Life Cycle.

Then,

Which of these, if any, did you think of before making the purchase?

What have you discovered about the purchase itself after considering the questions?

What did you discover about yourself and your values?

How many of these answers did you know?

Which answers are unknown, unclear, or maybe even somehow secret?

A Practical Handbook for Moral Growth   44

PATHS AND CHOICES

All human conditions are woven around with means and ends; goals and choices; influences on others and from others; and personal, family, community, and national histories, philosophies, religions, and cultures. No one is alone and unconnected. Examining our common paths helps us be aware of the choices and consequences we are creating.

Yet looking at ourselves as individuals is not enough. How do individuals interact and influence each other? What are the choices for moral Growth or Decay in the family, schools, community, state, and nation?

3.0.0   Paths in the Family

The first and most lasting influence on individuals is the extended family group. Families set up expectations and behavior patterns. In our families we learn how humans interact. We learn what our place in the world is and how we should relate to others. We learn how to use language and how to read emotional responses. As we venture out into the world, we continue to judge it and the people around us based on the primary attitudes and behaviors we learned "at our mother's knee." We can change, but it is hard.

3.1.0   Contagion and Needs for Growth or Decay

Moral Growth and Decay have specific characteristics, and these characteristics are contagious, passed on to others like a virus. A virus is invisible, easily passed on, even by just touching something the contagious person has touched. A virus can be passed on through the air by a breath, by nearness. As the doctor often says, if your sickness is caused by a virus, maybe some of the symptoms can be controlled, but there is no medicine to cure it. Stay home when you are contagious. You just have to rest and recuperate using your own inherent strength.

The thoughts and actions characteristic of moral Growth and moral Decay are contagious too. We don't have to like this—the fact is simply the fact. So how shall we pass on the characteristics of Growth and health? How shall we avoid or fight off the characteristics of Decay and death?

Consider these lists [see 2.3.5]:

Needs for Moral Growth and Health
- Direct, human relations
- Warm affectionate contacts
- Freedom to make choices
- Examples of inner harmony and strength
- Examples of the "art of living"
- Stimulating and interesting life

Needs for Moral Decay and Death
- Lack of human contact or influence of death-loving people
- Threats (physical, mental, or spiritual)
- Mechanical, rigid order
- Fright
- Lack of stimulation

Maybe we wonder how these can be contagious.

But really, how can they not be contagious?

Tone, gesture, and atmosphere contribute to the dynamics of relationships of all types. They help create courage or fear. They contribute to our degree of self-knowledge. They encourage intellectual, physical, and spiritual development—or discourage intellectual, physical, and spiritual development.

Imagine yourself as a child-soldier, intimidated and threatened into killing in order to live. Imagine being shut in a closet, being beaten for reading or learning, being degraded into unthinking obedience—how would you escape? How would you escape, not just physically—how would you escape emotionally, intellectually, and spiritually from this "death trap"? How have you or people you know escaped from threats, fright, or bad influences?

3.1.1 *Thought Experiment: Influences*

Think of specific people of any age who show unusual or striking characteristics, causes, or effects of moral Growth or moral Decay (see 2.1.0).

Do you know of any influences on them that might have contributed to who they are, for better or worse?

How would you describe the effect of their tone of voice, their style of gestures, and the general atmosphere surrounding them?

Are they "contagious"?

3.2.0　Parenting

Analysis and discussion of effective parenting seem unending in modern culture. Maybe this is partly because our extended families are often no longer sources of advice. Maybe we feel a mental or psychological dissonance about our required responsibility to guide and protect our families. Maybe an underlying and unexamined fear drives us. Perhaps it would be helpful to attempt a practical and concrete examination of what direction we could choose to go as parents and the means we can use to get to our imagined goal.

Do we want our children to Grow or Decay? This may seem like a foolish question. But it is not. Should our children be "better" than we are or "better off" than we are? What does that mean exactly? Often our greatest desire is to become wealthy, to have power or celebrity, or to own things and people. We are wishing for Decay. We may say—I just want my children to be happy or I just want my children to be successful—but in our minds happiness and success equal owning things, having power to make demands, or being rich and famous. Is that our real wish for our children?

The model of moral Growth and Decay seems to me to be one of the simplest ways of discussing parenting. Also because of its basic simplicity, it is one of the most effective explanations of various causes and effects in parenting.

3.2.1   *Thought Experiment: Parenting Styles*

These are widely used characteristics of parenting styles and the results of those styles in children.

Examine why each specific set of parental attitudes and behaviors might lead to those specific consequences in the child's attitudes and behaviors?

Think of real-world examples where these descriptions are true or false.

Many of the descriptions are "loaded" words—what do they mean?

What is an "excellent," "good," "average," or "poor" student in this context?

What do "problem-solving," "well-behaved," "whiny," or "inappropriate" mean?

Authoritative Parent:

 Affectionate and engaged

 Sets limits and enforces consequences

 Uses reason, logic, and appropriate negotiation

 Empowers a child's decision-making

A Practical Handbook for Moral Growth   48

So the child is likely to be

    Happy, responsible, and kind

    Good at problem-solving

    Self-motivated and confident

    Cooperative

    An excellent student

    A leader

Authoritarian Parent:

    Emotionally aloof

    Bossy and likely to say, "Because I said so"

    Uses physical punishment or verbal insults

        (psychological/emotional punishment)

    Dismisses a child's feelings

So the child is likely to be

    Moody and anxious

    Well-behaved

    An average to good student

    A follower

Permissive Parent:

    Affectionate

    Anxious to please and ends every sentence by asking, "Okay?"

    Indulgent

    Can't say no and stick to it

    Easily manipulated

So the child is likely to be

    Demanding and whiny

    Easily frustrated

    Lacking kindness and empathy

    A poor to average student

    A follower

Passive Parent:

 Emotionally removed or indifferent

 Uninvolved

 Abdicates discipline

 Inconsistent and unpredictable

So the child is likely to be

 Clingy and needy

 Inappropriate and rude

 Likely to get into trouble

 A poor student

 A follower

Clearly the "Authoritative Parent" is most likely to both be an example of moral Growth and also have a child who exhibits many of the characteristics of Growth, especially those connected to independence. This child is also likely to accept the processes of life and the frustrations of making an effort as well as to understand equity and reciprocity in relationships.

3.2.2 *Thought Experiment: Family Growth*

If a family wants to encourage Growth in the children, what would the adults in that family need to do to provide examples?

Think of specific actions and also unconscious behaviors or attitudes in adults that would demonstrate love of life

  demonstrate love of others and living things

  demonstrate responsible independence and freedom

Think of specific actions and also unconscious behaviors or attitudes in adults that would discourage fascination with non-life (death, force, violence, mechanism)

  discourage obsessive self-centeredness

  discourage irresponsibility or extreme dependence on others

A Practical Handbook for Moral Growth 50

3.2.3 *Thought Experiment: Getting Out of the Self*

Getting out of the self leads to Growth, but focus on the self to the exclusion of others leads to Decay. Doctors working with those suffering from depression often use medical interventions, but cognitive therapists also recommend retraining the mind to focus outside of the self in order to regain the habits of emotional and mental health. Adult companions of children model what it means to be human by example in their every word and deed, in their tone of voice and their gestures, and in the atmosphere surrounding them.

How can adults show the children around them examples of getting out of themselves and seeing others as real?

What attitudes and behaviors can be examples of seeing our neighbors to be as real as ourselves?

What attitudes and behaviors can be examples of seeing strangers, including those who are far away or who seem to be entirely different, to be just as human as ourselves?

What attitudes and behaviors can be examples of seeing nature and other life as a form of reality that humans need to respect?

3.2.4 Rachel Carson's "Sense of Wonder"

The natural world is also alive! Love of life and getting out of the self involves more than connecting to other humans, whether family, friends, neighbors, or strangers. Rachel Carson argues that showing young children the sense of wonder by example is more important than teaching them facts. She says that a sense of wonder needs to be "so indestructible that it [lasts] throughout life, as an unfailing antidote against the boredom and disenchantments of later years, the sterile preoccupation with things that are artificial, the alienation from the sources of our strength."

Her belief is that an adult companion of a child should share "the joy, excitement and mystery of the world we live in" even though he or she may not have all the facts: "If facts are the seeds that later produce knowledge and wisdom, then the emotions and the impressions of the senses are the fertile soil in which the seeds must grow. The years of early childhood are the time to prepare the soil. Once the emotions have been aroused—a sense of the beautiful, the excitement of the new and the unknown, a feeling of sympathy, pity, admiration or love—then we wish for knowledge about the object of our emotional response."

Carson says the sense of wonder comes from being receptive and aware of the sense of awe into adulthood: "Those who dwell, as scientists or laymen, among the beauties and mysteries of the earth are never alone or weary of life. Whatever the vexations or concerns of their personal lives, their thoughts can find paths that lead to inner contentment and to renewed excitement in living. Those who contemplate the beauty of the earth find reserves of strength that will endure as long as life lasts."

4.0.0   Paths in Education

If we actually want children to learn the attitudes and behaviors of moral Growth, then our system of education needs to choose them and act deliberately to foster them. This can be no accident. Every family, school, culture, religion, community, state, or nation teaches specific values and expectations—whether consciously or unconsciously. Often the path to moral Decay is easy to find by accident. But Decay may also be deliberately taught to us or rewarded by those who wish for and need dependent, fearful, helpless, obedient followers. Not thinking at all or letting someone else think for us is certainly easier than thinking, choosing, or acting for ourselves. Decay

A Practical Handbook for Moral Growth 52

is necessary for oligarchies, dictatorships, and totalitarian systems. But Decay destroys the essential strengths needed for a democratic form of government.

4.1.0   Public Education

Public education is the foundation of a democracy because democracy is based on all of the people, on their skills and knowledge, on their choices and actions. The more powerful small, select groups get, the less likely it is that the majority will be expected, required, even forced to make these important choices. Someone else will do it. Someone else will know. Someone else will choose. Someone else will think. This easy path leads to helplessness and hopelessness, passivity and ignorance, authoritarian control, and in the end loss of democracy itself. Public schools must actively choose to teach, guide, encourage, even "force," students toward moral Growth—because Decay means death to a democracy.

4.1.1   Teaching Styles

If the authoritative style of parenting is more likely to exhibit and result in the characteristics of moral Growth, how about teaching styles and methods? Paraphrasing some of the previous parenting behaviors and consequences to apply to teaching and learning might look like this:

- An **authoritative teacher** is affectionate and engaged; sets limits and enforces consequences; uses reason, logic, and appropriate negotiation; and empowers a student's decision-making so that the student is more likely to be happy, responsible, and kind; good at problem-solving; self-motivated and confident; cooperative; an excellent student; and a leader.

- An **authoritarian teacher** is emotionally aloof; is bossy and likely to say "because I said so"; uses physical punishments or verbal insults; and dismisses a student's feelings so that the student is more likely to be moody and anxious; well-behaved; an average to good student; and a follower.
- A **permissive teacher** is affectionate; is anxious to please and ends many sentences by asking "Okay?"; is indulgent; can't say no and stick to it; and is easily manipulated so that the student is likely to be demanding and whiny; easily frustrated; lacking kindness and empathy; a poor to average student; and a follower.
- A **passive teacher** is emotionally removed or indifferent; is uninvolved; abdicates discipline; and is inconsistent and unpredictable so that the student is clingy and needy; inappropriate and rude; likely to get into trouble; a poor student; and a follower.

4.1.2 *Thought Experiment: Teacher-Student Cause-Effect*
Consider the parent/teacher causes and child/student effects in the list above.
Do they have a basis in actual and practical everyday life?
How have you seen them in action among teachers and students?

Children learn how to parent by watching their parents in action. Students learn how to teach or mentor by watching their teachers in action. Workers learn how to supervise by watching their supervisors in action. Soldiers and citizens learn how to lead by watching their leaders in action. What are the principles we want to pass on to the next generation of parents, teachers, supervisors, and leaders?

We are the example of what the future will look like.

4.1.3 *Thought Experiment: Boss-Worker, Mentor-Learner, President-Citizen Cause-Effect*

Experiment with changing the words parent/teacher to boss or supervisor or CEO, mentor, guard or police, captain, bureaucrat or mayor or president and then change the words child/student to worker, learner, prisoner, soldier, or citizen.
What do you think strengthens or weakens this cause-effect relationship?
What do you think and feel about these ideas when you first see them?
What is the difference between authoritative and authoritarian leaders?

4.1.4 *Thought Experiment: Goals for Teaching*

In educational situations, specific thoughts, tones of voice, gestures, words, and deeds can lead to Growth or Decay. Learning Growth often requires intentional focus—Decay seems to come more easily because it requires less attention and effort. Of course, this process also depends on what attitudes and behaviors the child or student brings into the classroom from the home and family.

We are all sometimes in positions of teaching.
Consider a time when you taught someone, maybe a child, a coworker, a family member, or a friend.
What were your immediate and obvious goals?
How could your goals have expanded to include Growth?

4.1.5 Analysis: Why do these help Growth? How can they be made real?

These are some skills for Growth that can be added to any educational situation. As you examine these, try to "dissect" each one of the possibilities for Growth. Why is the thought or action important or useful in order to achieve Growth? Even though moral Growth and Decay are usually learned by example and not taught explicitly— how might Growth be consciously encouraged inside any form of educational system? How can these thoughts or actions be shown by example and understood, encouraged, or rewarded in the practical realities of a classroom, lesson plan, or larger curriculum? If you teach or mentor anyone of any age, why and how could you use the principles that lead to Growth?

Teaching the art of living—why and how?
> Respect for all
> Justice for all
> Dignity for all
> Independence
> Responsibility

Providing stimulating and interesting life examples within the total curriculum—why and how?
> Reading
> Speaking
> Writing
> Mathematics
> Social or behavioral studies
> Economics
> History and geography
> Sciences, including earth/nature studies
> Physical education
> Art
> Music

Providing opportunities to "get out of the self"—why and how?
> Helping individual others
> Mentoring and being mentored by all ages—
>> young and old(er) working together
>> adult volunteers as examples
> Helping the community

A Practical Handbook for Moral Growth

Helping the natural world

Creating an atmosphere of warmth and affection—why and how?
Encouraging acceptance and kindness within the entire learning community
Creating a welcoming and friendly atmosphere
Promoting thoughtfulness and preventing the use of children or learners as means to an end or as objects
Encouraging appropriate affection and preventing the sexualizing of children/learners
Accepting each child/learner as valuable in his or her own right and reducing the manipulation of children/learners for economic gain
Encouraging mutual helpfulness and patience

Providing examples of inner harmony and strength—why and how?
Encouraging self-discipline
Encouraging balanced perspectives on problems

Providing examples and studying how to use critical thinking—why and how?
Understanding reasoning and logic
Analyzing choices and consequences
Sorting out and analyzing "facts" and how to use them
Understanding cause and effect
Understanding the differences among
--facts (pieces of information)
--interpretations (what the facts mean)
--applications (what the facts and interpretations mean to me)

Providing security—why and how?
Eliminating threats and fright among students, between adults and children, or between teacher and learner

Creating an atmosphere of calmness and joy

Establishing equal and uniform safety for all

Establishing equal and uniform consideration for others

Encouraging personal responsibility—why and how?

Explaining and allowing for choices

Explaining and allowing for responsible use of freedom

Explaining and allowing for <u>both</u> successes and failures in achieving goals

Understanding the real alternatives and the moment of choice—why and how?

Showing how to overcome frustrations

Practicing how to use personal will and effort to achieve a goal

Recognizing the context (circumstances) and subtexts (underlying assumptions) of life—why and how?

Studying current events that are appropriate to each age

Studying other places in the world in order to understand and care about the stranger as a person

Analyzing how choices and assumptions (conscious and unconscious) work toward actions and decisions

Analyzing how the natural world affects the human-made world

Analyzing how the human-made world affects the natural world

4.1.6 *Thought Experiment:*
Doing More than One Thing with Multiple Goals

Because it is never actually possible to do only "one" thing at a time, how can parents, teachers, leaders, and mentors use activities to serve multiple purposes?

A Practical Handbook for Moral Growth

Why have multiple goals or purposes for every action, discussion, or learning process?
How can this be done in a practical way in the normal course of life?
Think of multiple "lessons" in one activity.

Using skills and tools for multiple purposes
> For example:
> Performance and speech
> Physical education and sports
> Music and dance
> Art
> Literature and writing
> Maps and geography

Integrating home and school
> Examples of caring about your neighbor that can be practiced at home
> Examples of helping children help, both within and outside the family
> Teaching children to teach—not just letting them try, but also showing them how to teach effectively. (Teaching methods and goals should not be a secret.)
> Explaining how Growth works and what goals are helpful and useful

Observation of nature in specific, concrete form leads to understanding the local reality as well as general information from far away.
> Local weather
> Local plants
> Local animals

5.0.0   Paths in Local Community

Knowing and understanding our place in the world feels like such a strange expectation in an "advanced" modern society. Often the local community hardly exists, except perhaps in the context of high school sports or specialized groups with common interests, such as religious or business organizations or social groups. Supporting our locally and independently owned businesses seems somehow out of step with the global economy. We feel an unexamined need to fit into the widely advertised sources of power and fashion and celebrity. Most of us have forgotten how to grow our own food or make our own clothes. Our cars and appliances are designed to be impossible for us to maintain or fix. Often when our paychecks are deposited directly into our various accounts, we lose track of how the taxes or insurance actually work. We have vague expectations for these things, but no real understanding of where or how the taxes are used and no idea of how or why the health care system functions, or doesn't function. Someone else is "taking care" of that for us—we hope.

5.1.0   Citizenship

Many opportunities for Growth can exist in our communities. Groups larger than our individual families can reinforce loving others, including neighbors, strangers, and nature. The community can offer opportunities for a stimulating, interesting life, for taking action, and for cooperating with many others for the common good. In fact, the community is an important site for the "common good." Inside the family and even inside the classroom, it is relatively easy to recognize what the common good might be, but as we move outward in our relationships and duties, this common good naturally becomes more theoretical. Understanding the cause-effect and logic of the common good is an important step "out of the self" and into the world. The first place this kind of step occurs for most of us is in our local neighborhoods and communities.

In a democracy, the people can have many opportunities for self-direction and self-organization. In fact, that is the very thing that struck Alexis de Tocqueville when he visited the new United States of America in 1831. In <u>Democracy in America</u> (1835) he describes the processes of democracy in action as arising from community organizing efforts, the training ground of local citizens and leaders. After this local experimentation and practice, democracy eventually can grow up to be a wider regional, state, and national system because the citizens are both willing and able to take responsibility and exercise freedom of choice. It may be that in our current centralized and bureaucratized version of large-scale government and institutions, we as individuals have lost these skills and need to rediscover them, practice them at the local level, and once again bring them upwards in the system for the good of the whole.

The grassroots is the most powerful source of strength in a democratic system. Small groups are effective not because the participants are professional or have excellent skills, but because more people can have the experience and practice of leadership in a wider variety of ways. Historically this was done in a myriad of small towns and small schools across the nation. In small schools almost everyone sang in the choir <u>and</u> played on sports teams <u>and</u> participated in the school play <u>and</u> was some sort of leader in a small group. With 25 or 50 students in the senior class, virtually no one could sit out. Now because the population is clustered into cities and huge schools that are supposed to provide economies of scale, fewer and fewer individual adults or children have the opportunity to learn and develop unexpected skills and to participate in a wide range of experiences. Only the best 10 of the 500 boys in the senior high school can play on the varsity basketball team. Only the best 150 students out of 1500 can play in a band. Perhaps more important, we no longer understand that sometimes we just help because we are needed—because everyone is needed. In a giant system we are tempted to forget that everyone can do something and that everyone needs to be needed.

5.1.1 Thought Experiment: Local Opportunities for Growth

List some opportunities in your community or neighborhood that could be helpful for Growth, both for individual people or families and for the strengthening of the community itself.
How could they be encouraged?
Who should encourage them?

5.1.2 Thought Experiment: Local Responsibilities

Local responsibilities can be effectively done only by local citizens. Using local volunteers spreads out the leadership experiences, responsibility, and tasks. When this happens, no one person is burned out and everyone can stretch their skills and learn new ones.
Where in your local community or neighborhood are these responsibilities being met?
Who is doing the organizing and leading?

- Understanding the local bioregion
- Finding sources of local food and providing farmers' markets
- Promoting locally created and distributed energy (such as solar rooftops and local wind, water, manure/methane, biomass, co-generation, etc.)

- Responsibility for local beauty and order
- Responsibility for safety in neighborhoods
- Responsibility for neighborliness, mutual help, and helping the helpless

- Creating local music

A Practical Handbook for Moral Growth   62

- Creating local sports of all types
- Creating local art
- Creating local traditions and community events

- Using local resources in cooperative groups, including churches, synagogues, and mosques, to meet community needs
- Using local schools or colleges as activity centers and meeting places
- Using local business to keep money circulating in the community, to support neighbors, and to provide local jobs
- Using local libraries for community education, issue outreach, and discussion groups
- Using local counseling resources to prevent violence, fear, and threat

5.2.0   Leadership

Local leaders who have arisen in community groups have the power to help create a healthy community. Leaders can encourage—
- exercising independent thought and analysis
- making choices with the common good of the whole community in mind
- using freedom wisely
- having the courage to take a risk in leadership or in helping others
- taking personal responsibility for the work of making a community function as a whole

The members of a community need to be willing and able to take personal responsibility. To succeed in this, a contagious tone and atmosphere for Growth must pervade all the citizens. Sometimes it is easier for local leaders to require obedience, to object to citizens' requests for information or transparency, or to take power themselves because no one else can do it right. When this happens, an atmosphere of fear or threat and feelings of incompetence spread and infect citizens. Helping others help themselves is more difficult than doing it for them, but it is more effective for the health and well being of the community as a whole and provides for the development of future leaders.

5.2.1. Qualities of a Leader

In Lao-tzu's Tao Te Ching (#17) the qualities of leadership are explored. Lao-tzu recommends the "invisible" leader who creates or designs the possibilities for citizens to act and then allows that productive action:

The best leader is one whose existence is barely known by the people.
Next comes one whom they love and praise.
Next comes one they fear.
Next comes one they defy.
If you do not trust enough, you will not be trusted.
(The Tao: The Sacred Way #17, Ed. Tolbert McCarroll)

The Master doesn't talk, he acts.
When his work is done,
the people say, "Amazing:
we did it, all by ourselves!"
(Tao Te Ching #17, Trans. Stephen Mitchell)

Sometimes in an emergency the people may need to be given a fish, but as immediately as possible they need to know how to fish, how to create their own equipment, and how to care for their own fishery. The primary responsibility of the leader is to create and organize the processes for everyone to make the equipment, get the training, and practice the skill. Using their freedom, power, and personal responsibility, the people can fish for themselves. The leader facilitates, and the people act. New leaders arise. The community becomes vibrant and healthy when everyone, women and men, young and old, have a productive part in doing good and necessary work.

6.0.0   Paths in the State/Province/Region

If we ask ourselves what responsibilities have been given to the local and state governments in the United States Constitution, we might come up with a list that includes public education, a local and state justice and prison system, some local and state oversight of economics and taxation, and creation and maintenance of infrastructure for the common use.

6.1.0   Education

Sometimes we are tempted to consider education to be the same as practical skill development or job training. This essentially reduces the human being and the citizen to a cog in the economic machine. Surely being human means more than only earning a living. Being a citizen means more than fitting in and following the rules. The purpose of public education in a democracy includes training, but involves much more.

Religious education may be designed to create believers who follow the theologically approved paths and think approved thoughts. Education in a dictatorship may be training in obedience to the authoritarian system. But a democracy cannot function without informed, responsible citizens who care about and respect each other. A democracy requires independent, thinking citizens who are willing and able to exercise freedom wisely and make choices intelligently.

6.1.1 *Thought Experiment: Defining Public Education*

Define public education.
What is included in a good education?
Why should specific topics and/or skills be taught?
Just as important, what attitudes should result from a good education?
What behaviors should result from a good education?

6.1.2 Education to Encourage Growth in a Democracy

One purpose of education needs to be encouraging moral Growth rather than Decay so that a society can not only survive economically, but also prosper as a just and stimulating community. It also seems that some reasonable hopes in designing a public education system would include skills, attitudes, and behaviors for democratic citizenship. Such a system can help create citizens of a democracy, rather than just obedient robots for an authoritarian system or helpless consumers with no sense of their personal freedoms and no understanding of responsible choices.

The goals of education that encourages Growth would include—

- Educating citizens to understand how to make responsible personal choices
- Educating citizens to recognize and understand the immediate and long-term consequences of their choices
- Educating citizens to recognize healthy leaders and to be leaders themselves
- Supporting a stimulating and interesting life and Growth for all ages
- Providing skills and tools for individual thinking and acting
- Providing information and experiences that lead to productive, healthy relationships with others

A Practical Handbook for Moral Growth 66

- Providing information and experiences that lead to love of life and care for the natural world
- Providing information and experiences that lead to a productive and useful life of economic sufficiency and psychic abundance

6.1.3 Using Resources Effectively

Public resources can be used in many ways, but where would they make the most difference for the most citizens? Experience has shown that building from the bottom up is stronger and more efficient than trying to impose a system of behavior or a set of rules or a list of specific actions from the top down.

Spending money on early childhood and family education, preschool, and elementary school is effective and efficient. If we don't spend resources here, then we can spend money later on prisons. Prisons often are where we lock away those who never learned how to have healthy relationships, who never learned to choose productive actions, or who never learned the power of personal responsibility. Of course, some citizens may be lost to abuses of power, some may be afflicted with severe mental illness, and some may be so trained in violence and fear that they cannot be drawn back. Society does have to be protected from predators and criminals. But resources are best used to support Growth from the beginning of life, rather than fighting inevitable Decay later. If the need for Growth is ignored, then Decay will be contagious in families and communities. It will multiply and infect us all. We need to provide the resources for Growth in early life.

State and community resources should be used for positive experiences, skills, and information. The first government responsibility is for educational infrastructure, such as schools and libraries. Models of Growth in teachers and mentors can be trained and supported. A democracy needs to spend its educational resources first for the youngest children and their families. Then resources should be used for K-12, including strong high school programs. The next level of need is for community colleges where those who have fallen through the cracks can try again or where those with the fewest personal resources can be provided with an opportunity to grow and learn. And finally state colleges and universities are needed where those who have developed strong skills throughout their earlier years can do advanced work. These steps will lead to productive, creative leaders and citizens. Those who are prepared through early life will have the personal strength, skills, and abilities to love, respect, and care for their world as productive human beings and citizens. They will be both able and willing to provide the personal and monetary resources for the next generations.

6.2.0   Justice and Equity in a Democracy

Another need for local and state resources includes a system of laws and justice and, when necessary, a system of punishment.

6.2.1   *Thought Experiment: Defining Justice*
How would you describe justice?
What are the characteristics of a just community?
What are the external signs of a just society?
What is the meaning of a just government?
What is injustice?
How is justice related to law?
Is legal vs. illegal the same as just vs. unjust?

6.2.2.   Characteristics of Justice

A Practical Handbook for Moral Growth   68

The Reverend Dr. Martin Luther King in his "Letter from the Birmingham Jail" comments on the difference between *legal* and *illegal* as opposed to *just* and *unjust*. His argument is that the laws of a specific society depend on who is in charge—Hitler designed the laws so that the Holocaust in Nazi Germany was legal. Would you consider *legal* to be the same as *just*? What is justice? Often the actions coming out of a corrupt corporation or institution are legal, but are they honest? What is the difference between *legal* and *honest*?

If we reconsider the characteristics of Growth and the characteristics of Decay, we can make some general observations about justice.

- The same rules need to apply to all, with no division by class or race or religion or place, because there is no such thing as justice for only one group—justice must be equal.
- Justice means defending and empowering the powerless against misuse by the powerful.
- The stability and equality of the rule of law is essential.
- Fairness in the courts and in the application of rules and laws is required.
- The powerful must be prevented from gaining special favors and from misusing the weak, no matter what the source of the power difference (age; gender; race; economic or social class).
- Punishment must follow immediately for real harm against individuals and society, but threat or fear of punishment must not be used as a means of enforcing unequal power.
- Justice is an active choice for a society and is not possible if the people are passive.
- Justice means eliminating threats, fright, and fear in everyday life.
- True justice means eliminating the causes as well as effects of Decay.
- Justice includes security for the future that makes Growth possible.

6.2.3 *Thought Experiment: Justice in Action*

Considering these characteristics, how would you improve justice in your family, community, and state?

How would you improve justice in your work and in the institutions that surround you?

How would you improve justice in the nation?

How would you improve justice in the world?

6.3.0 Prisons

6.3.1. *Thought Experiment: Growth in Prison?*

If you were in prison (by your own fault) and wanted to change, what would you want or need?

If you had been raised surrounded by moral Decay and wanted moral Growth instead, what would you want or need?

If you couldn't read or write or do math, what would help you?

If you had no useful skills for supporting yourself, what would you need to survive outside prison?

6.3.2 Purpose of Prison

Assuming that the purpose of prison is to make society safer, the first goal is to eliminate some of the causes of bad choices rather than just punishing the effects. If society's only purpose for prisons is revenge and punishment, then it is focusing on the short term release of anger rather than on long term usefulness and logic. Increasing moral Decay in a society, including for those temporarily behind bars, inevitably has long term negative effects for the prisoners and their families and their eventual neighbors in society. The negative effects also spread to the justice system itself and everyone connected to the prison system.

A Practical Handbook for Moral Growth   70

6.3.3   Suggestions for Change

None of the following suggestions have much monetary influence on the system's costs (except maybe to reduce the costs coming from anger, violence, and fear). The instinctual reasons against doing these things are that we want the prisoner to suffer, to be miserable, to be afraid, to have a rotten life—just as rotten a life as those who have been his or her victims want in retribution. This person caused fear and suffering, caused pain and humiliation, so why not give him or her a taste of that medicine? Victims of crimes have every right to want this retribution. Unfortunately, this anger, violence, fear, misery, and suffering will be brought out of prison and into others' lives yet again. Then we will probably once again punish the criminal rather than trying to eliminate the crime. Inevitably Decay will threaten and infect all of us over and over again.

No doubt you can think of suggestions to encourage the possibility of moral Growth. Here are some examples of possible changes that would do no harm, might have a chance of helping, and would cost little to virtually nothing. They would be worth the experiment. It may be that our prisons need to be divided more closely into "communities" of those in various stages of Growth or Decay so that some at least may be given a chance to "escape" from Decay.

- Providing basic education in reading, writing, and mathematics as well as providing a library is relatively simple and has important long-term effects on a prisoner's chances in life. Paying those prisoners who can read or do math to mentor those who can't is just as useful as paying them their 25 cents to do laundry or clean floors and may stimulate them to do more advanced learning for themselves. We send books to Africa as a charity, so we could just as easily send books to prisons as a charity.

- Providing examples of a stimulating, interesting life is simple if we just use public television and public radio, documentaries, and educational films of all types, including educational cartoons—available by closed circuit in cells, if necessary. It is easy to eliminate "entertainment" that glorifies Decay and violence. We can eliminate pornography and violent movies because the prison can control what is available. If this is suffering for some types of prisoners, then that would be fine—let them suffer by gaining information and education. If watching public television or listening to public radio is punishment, then so be it. Most of the little educational and thoughtful programming in our society is found on public outlets or cable television channels focused on science, history, or education. Since reading is often a problem, this form of pastime would at least have some possible long-term use, certainly more than doing and thinking nothing.

- Trying to change the tone, gesture, and atmosphere to one of calmness might encourage moral Growth rather than Decay. Allowing prisoners to learn to draw or paint, to play instruments, to perform theater, or to learn gardening has value beyond just an interesting yet calming atmosphere. These things give those who are agitated, angry, and fearful a new outlet and way of dealing with problems that can carry over into post-prison life. Further, playing Baroque and Classical instrumental music changes the entire atmosphere of a place in ways that are almost unimaginable to those who have never watched the effects. Perhaps we believe that beauty or fine music or art should be reserved for those who deserve it? But maybe that is actually part of the problem. Maybe we really should try a flower on the table.

- Exercise dissipates tension, but the exercise can be yoga and tai chi. Meditation also dissipates tension. Weight lifting doesn't have to be the only prison exercise. Exercise doesn't have to mean

A Practical Handbook for Moral Growth 72

methods of doing more harm. Martial arts have advantages because they can encourage self-discipline and respect, but only in strictly controlled settings or as rewards for beneficial changes in behavior. Competitive sports are fun, provided the players have learned to "play well with others."

- Giving some opportunity for small groups with common interests to study or work together might be useful as a way to encourage socialization skills, desire to learn, feelings of value, and interest in the natural world. Gardening for food like fruit and vegetables to supplement prison needs or to donate to charity could be an outlet for energy as well as a source of useful information and skills. Small groups can study nature that comes from beyond the prison walls, like flowers, butterflies, or birds, and even do simple experiments for scientists. Helper dogs can be trained to be given to those in need.

- Psychological and social counseling can be helpful, and rehabilitation from drug addiction is essential to Growth. We need to analyze what behaviors are the most essential for Growth and reintegration into society. Then we can design ways of teaching and reinforcing those specific behaviors before releasing prisoners into the general public. Of course, it is extremely difficult to help someone whose life-long habits are all on the side of Decay to become a loving, caring, responsible, productive member of a community (which is why spending our social capital on the young is so much more efficient), but still the community needs to try— both to help the prisoner and to protect society in the future.

6.3.4 *Thought Experiment, one more time: What Would You Need?*

If you were in prison, if you were surrounded by Decay, but wanted to change, what would you want or need to help you?
How could you make choices tending toward love of life?
How could you learn to love or respect yourself, others around you, strangers?
How could you learn to love nature and living things?
How could you learn independence and responsibility?
How could you learn to handle freedom?

6.4.0 Reversing or Preventing Decay

Clearly we as a society cannot just focus on creating opportunities, examples, and an atmosphere that fosters Growth. Individuals and communities have to consciously work to reverse Decay. Reversing Decay often means changing long established behaviors and ways of thinking. Helping children means helping parents, teachers, and mentors. This is not an easy process because un-learning habits of thought and action can be painful—emotionally, mentally, and even physically. For those who have gone so far into Decay that they find themselves in crime or in prisons, this can be intensely difficult. But the danger is greater than that, for those who find themselves in positions of virtually unlimited power are in just as great a danger. Anyone can fall into habits of Decay, sometimes in the most extreme sense of personal and moral rot.

6.4.1 Lessons from the Stanford Prison Experiment: The Dangers of Unlimited Power

Philip Zimbardo, a social psychologist at Stanford University, organized what was called the Stanford Prison Experiment in 1971. The purpose of this experiment was to study the psychology of evil, violence, torture, and terrorism by creating conditions for abuse. Ordinary university students played the roles of both prisoners and guards in a realistic setting. The results of the experiment were clear within a few days. After less than a week, it was halted because the emotional transformations became too painful. Observation showed that the situation itself quickly changed the students' normal characters, so they actually began to think and behave like the pathologically passive or angry prisoner or the abusive guard. Just examining the design of the experiment will remind anyone of easily recognizable methods used by totalitarian governments.

Even though the students did not actually physically harm each other, the use of threat and the design of the experiment were enough to change the way the students thought and acted. Costumes created a feeling of being anonymous and not personally responsible in both the prisoners and the guards. The military style uniform with reflective sunglasses created the illusion of power. Nakedness, masks, or prison smocks reinforced powerlessness. Among those who acted in power positions, anonymity and lack of personal accountability lead to antisocial behavior. Those who were costumed to appear part of an undifferentiated and inhuman mass and who were treated as powerless actually did become passive, accepting their fate. Some were filled with rage and rebellion in a matter of days.

These costumes erased the individual as an individual. Erasing individualism took away personal responsibility for the proper use of power. It also took away personal human dignity. Compare this experimental situation to pictures of Abu Ghraib Prison in Iraq or to Nazi death camps or to the Soviet Gulag. Golding's The Lord of the Flies was an insightful observation of what happens to human nature without leadership or examples of moral Growth. When we lose ourselves as individuals, it is easy to fall into moral Decay.

Furthermore, the students' ability to reason and analyze was lost in the Stanford Prison Experiment. Emotions took over, and the students "in power" did not reflect on the causes or effects of their actions. According to Zimbardo, this "deindividuated state" changed the mental functions of <u>both</u> the powerful and the powerless, both the guards and the prisoners. In the experiment, problems with abuse became worse when no higher authority was in charge and also at night when no one seemed to be watching.

In a review of Zimbardo's recent analysis of the experiment, <u>The Lucifer Effect: Understanding How Good People Turn Evil</u> (2007), the reviewer argues, "We are best able to avoid, challenge, and change negative situational forces only by recognizing their potential to 'infect' us as they have others who were similarly situated" ["Think You're Above Doing Evil? Think Again," <u>Discover</u> Feb. 2007: 69]. These observations are essentially the same as Erich Fromm's observations in <u>The Heart of Man: Its Genius for Good and Evil</u>. They are also recognizable in current news or recent historical behavior in Bosnia, Kosovo, Rwanda, Sudan, or Burma, to name only a few examples. Reflecting on his experiences inside the Soviet prison system, Aleksandr Solzhenitsyn in <u>The Gulag Archipelago, 1918-1956</u> (1973) says "the line between good and evil is in the center of every human heart."

6.4.2   Requirements for Reversing Opportunities for Decay

Based on these observations, specific methods are needed to reverse this effect where ever there is a conflict between power and powerlessness. This could be in the home, in the school, in the community, in business, in the military, or in government, as well as in a prison. Every human relationship is potentially subject to these effects.

A leader for moral Growth is needed. According to Zimbardo's observations the requirements include—

A Practical Handbook for Moral Growth   76

- someone who is clearly in charge and willing to exercise authority, <u>and</u>
- who requires honorable behavior, <u>and</u>
- who challenges abuse of power, <u>and</u>
- who watches or pays attention.

Those in power positions must be trained to recognize lack of reason and lack of reflection in themselves and others who may have power (parents, teachers, police, supervisors or bosses, corporate officers, officials of all types). All of us also need to have examples to copy and personal beliefs that help us fight against the allure of power. What do we teach our children about the responsibilities of power of any type and the duty to resist abuse of that power?

Bullies can be any age—defenders of the weak can be any age—those with moral insight and courage can be any age.

6.4.3   *Thought Experiment:*
Dangers of the Use of Power

Analyze the use of power in the family, the school, the community or neighborhood, a business or corporation, an arm of government. Think of a situation in which power can be abused—the more real this might be in your own life the better.

How could Decay be prevented or reversed in a specific situation?

Who is in charge?

Are those in charge willing to exercise proper authority?

Do those in charge require honorable behavior?

Do those in charge challenge abuse of power?

Do those in charge pay attention to what is actually happening (watch)?

Growth requires good people to do something. Decay is much easier. As Edmund Burke said, "All that is necessary for the triumph of evil is that good men do nothing." In Leslie Silko's novel <u>Ceremony</u> the power of the "witches" is reduced as soon as someone is paying attention, noticing the existence of Decay—then "It is gone, for now." Decay is always waiting and ready to return, but it can be checked if we are both watching and willing to challenge it.

6.5.0　The Right Use of Power in Everyday Life

Let's consider this with respect to "oversight." A strong parallel naturally occurs between the Stanford prison experiment and many other forms of power because of the inherent conflicts in human nature. The characteristics of moral Growth and Decay do not just affect prisons and prisoners. Growth and Decay affect all of us in all of our everyday choices.

6.5.1　Need for Oversight

Henry David Thoreau in his essay "On the Duty of Civil Disobedience," says, "It is truly enough said, that a corporation has no conscience, but a corporation of conscientious [people] is a corporation *with* a conscience." Clearly he means that human choices, attitudes, and behaviors are what control our groups, large and small, for better or worse. And we need to take up our responsibility to speak for conscience, for moral Growth.

Of course, this responsibility is not easy. For example, consider the role of government in overseeing or controlling air and water pollution, or pharmaceutical efficacy and safety, or energy efficiency, or banking and investment honesty. Could we rely on self-control and self-monitoring in order to protect the air we all breathe and the water we all drink? Will manufacturers just naturally test and oversee the drugs we use or the machines we need? Will those who gather in our money exercise unquestioned honesty in our investments? Will people with power over deciding whether or how much to pollute, whether to do extensive drug safety tests, whether to make the most efficient products, or whether to be entirely honest with other people's money just "do the right thing"? What does your knowledge of history and human nature tell you?

History has shown us that while there are some exemplary and positive cases of independent self-control and self-monitoring at all levels of organizations, in the vast majority of cases depending <u>solely</u> on self-control and self-monitoring is unlikely to be either safe or effective for the majority of decisions. Normally the temptation to choose (or to order others to choose) the most profitable or easiest path is too great to withstand alone. Once again, the contagious example of the group in which all are tending toward Decay together is hard to resist, though not impossible.

This tendency toward Decay does not have to be caused by indifference to the health, safety, or property of others, although it might be. It doesn't have to be caused by dishonesty and greed, although it might be. Often it appears to be just a matter of choosing the most immediately profitable course for the business, the manufacturer, the corporation, or the firm.

To put the most charitable construction on it, perhaps choosing toward moral Decay is a failure of imagination so that no one else is even considered. The long term or widespread negative effects for others are ignored. Perhaps other people and their circumstances are not even real to the person who chooses an attitude or action that does harm or who issues orders or follows orders that will do harm. At every level of every organization there are questions of power. Whistleblowers or dissenters are usually persecuted, either officially or unofficially. Often the "watchers" who have the courage to speak are eliminated wherever possible, even though they are the very ones who are the most valuable to moral Growth.

6.5.2 Personal Oversight

Good leaders actively require honorable behavior, challenge abuse, and watch the actions of those whom they influence at all levels. This can be done either personally or through an established and accountable chain of command. But it needs to be done to ensure that the good of others, even the good of nature is taken into account. The larger the organization is, however, the greater the obstacles even the best leader might face.

How can a society organize itself to reduce this Decay and encourage Growth? How can we balance our condemnation of the "tattletale" or the "snitch" with our need for truth and responsibility? How can we recognize when the watcher is helpful and when the watcher is turning into just another spy for another form of abuse of authority? The watcher who is trying to enforce threats, fear, or violence or to eliminate independent thought can be a serious danger. But with no honest watchers and no honorable leaders and no dissenters, all hell breaks out.

These are essential questions that are strongly dependent on the power of moral Growth or the power of moral Decay in each individual, in groups of individuals, and in the society as a whole.

6.5.3 Transparency

Transparency is the safest course for the good of all. The cleansing power of sunshine is essential. What needs to be done in the dark or in secret is usually found to be wrong, embarrassing, or dishonorable. Having many objective watchers and many who challenge abuse and demand honest behavior is helpful to a society.

A Practical Handbook for Moral Growth   80

If the "watchers" give power to their representative government for the purpose of oversight and equity throughout the economic system, this can be efficient and effective. Yet, of course, the governmental bodies, committees, departments, and agencies also need our attention as citizens. The American government is uniquely set up with a balance of powers to try to accomplish this goal, but ultimately the citizens themselves must consistently demand transparency. Any one person or group or any power center that is exempt from transparency is in danger of falling or being lead into Decay, consciously or unconsciously.

Once again Thoreau has a crucial insight: "Why does [government] not encourage its citizens to be on the alert to point out its faults [. . .]? Why does it always crucify Christ, and excommunicate Copernicus and Luther, and pronounce Washington and Franklin rebels?" Those with strength of conscience need to be active in supporting moral Growth.

6.5.4   *Thought Experiment: Methods of Oversight*

Consider these questions in the light of this discussion of the forms and uses of power that we see all around us. Choose a specific situation in the family, the school, the community or neighborhood, businesses or corporations, or any level of government to use for analysis.

How could Decay be prevented or reversed if the processes in this situation were transparent?

How can outsiders (the public) encourage those in charge of a situation to be willing to exercise their authority to require honorable behavior?

How can outsiders (the public) encourage those in charge to watch for and challenge abuses of power?

How can insiders in this specific case encourage the process of Growth through honorable behavior for the good of all?

Why do we have such a problem accepting internal correction or a whistleblower in this situation?

How can errors in judgment be dealt with without destroying our freedom of action and invention or our sense of personal responsibility?

How can personal responsibility and independence be strengthened for the sake of Growth?

How can we eliminate the consciously dishonest and abusive who take advantage of our often unconscious shortsightedness or lack of imagination?

How can we encourage the watchers without becoming a society of "spies"?

6.6.0   Helping the Neighbor and the Stranger

Another use of state or local resources often goes toward helping the helpless. The first impetus for this process is, of course, the instinct to help one's family, friends, and neighbors when they are in need and cannot help themselves. We identify with them and their situations. Through their experience we can see the reality of ourselves in the same potential disasters. It is easy. We are close to them. By knowing them and their situations, we recognize how we can help in the best way. We step up to take in the orphan, to care for the sick, to contribute food to the hungry, or to offer clothing to the destitute because they are our family, friends, or neighbors.

When we give this responsibility to the local, state, or even national government and the larger bureaucracy steps into our shoes, we continue to hope that our contributions in tax money and our empowerment of the system will keep on "doing the right thing." Doing the right thing is doing what we ourselves would do. The advantage of the larger system might be a correspondingly larger and tighter safety net that would support everyone more equally, but the disadvantage might be a sense of impersonal and detached "help" without the human touch.

Another advantage is the wider sharing of responsibility, so that entire communities can be aided when all are in trouble together or so that those in trouble can be helped even though their immediate group can't or won't help them. A disadvantage might be a feeling of helplessness and disempowerment inside of a huge and impersonal system. Yet if someone has been disowned, who will help? Who will rescue the abandoned? Should the sick or hungry be left lying by the side of the road? Every community has to face these questions.

6.6.1 *Thought Experiment: Who Would Help?*

If you were in trouble, how would you want the system to help you?
How would you feel?
Whom would you reach out to?

6.6.2 Helping the Whole Person

As societies grow larger and more complex, we face increasing difficulty designing systems of help for those who need our assistance while also encouraging personal responsibility and wise uses of freedom and choice. Discussion and counseling can strengthen personal responsibility, freedom, and individual independence. As individuals and communities create Growth rather than Decay, people can be strengthened to help each other and to take responsibility whenever and wherever possible. But if there is to be an error, then erring on the side of love, caring, and respect is necessary for any community's moral Growth.

6.7.0 Taxes as Resources for the Common Good

Communities of all sizes use taxes to combine their resources for the common good. This makes choosing which needs are given which resources an inescapable and essential question.

In our culture, we can use the power of money through the tax system to reward ("incentivize") behaviors that lead to ethical Growth and reduce or eliminate ("disincentivize") behaviors that lead to ethical Decay if we think clearly and specifically about what we want and don't want as a society.

Some of us hope that "the invisible hand of the market" will take care of everything for us, so humans just have to stand back and let the market-magic work. Indeed, the free market has often done a good job of creating and distributing goods and services, but not without human oversight. The market, free or not, should not control us. Belief in a market economy can not be the same as being helpless and passive. Injustice and damage do not have to be inevitable just because the "hand" of the market has created or allowed them to exist. In a democracy the citizens are required to make choices about their lives and the laws by which they want to be governed. The market has no mind or heart or spirit. We need human decisions for human life. Choosing a non-human control mechanism or being passive in the face of inequitable "market forces" is an abdication of human responsibility.

In addition, a fictional "free" market regularly leaves control in the hands of the few, the most powerful and wealthy, who can manipulate it while everyone else stands by helplessly. Moral Growth cannot be passive. Freedom includes our finding the facts, deciding what they mean, and then acting to create a system that rewards justice, productive activity, competence, psychic abundance, usefulness, favorable development, and creativity. I need to know how my new shirt has affected others—who has gained and who or what has lost because of my particular choice. There is much more to know than the simple fact that my demand has been supplied by an invisible hand.

"What we see is not necessarily the whole truth any more than the tree we see above ground is the whole tree" (John Fowles). Seeing the tree above the ground is fairly simple if we are awake and alert, but we also need to recognize that the rest of the tree exists below ground. What is the whole tree like? Where are its roots? The corporation is, after all, a collection of people who make decisions. However, those decisions are not just made in the board room or the head office. Decisions are made at every step in a market economy. The market should be influenced and regulated by the human mind and heart. Even here moral Growth is possible.

6.7.1 *Thought Experiment:*
Taxes as Rewards and Punishments

What behaviors do you think we as a society should encourage?
What should we discourage?
Why should we use this power?

Pick a specific negative behavior that society at large needs to address: excessive energy use, air pollution, water pollution, waste disposal, for example.
What concrete, specific behavior or result do we want to reduce or eliminate?
Why do we want this?
Can the tax system get at it?
What specific actions should we take to "disincentivize" this behavior?

On the same issue—
What concrete, specific behavior or result do we want to encourage and reward?
Why do we want this?
Can the tax system get at it?

What specific actions should we take to "incentivize" this behavior?

6.7.2 The Purposes and Effects of a Tax System

A complex, organizationally centralized society uses what we hope is an equitable tax structure to cover the costs of the burdens we have agreed to bear as a society. We use taxes to maintain our community life and our mutual infrastructure. We all realize that police and fire protection, a road and transportation system, an effective and available public education system, a uniform way of providing a safety net for the needy, a safe and sanitary water and sewage system, and a leadership structure to help us face immediate threats and long term planning are all needed. We recognize the value of the common good as well as the reality of common needs. While recognizing our individualism and our freedom, we have also banded together to solve mutual problems and contribute toward mutual necessities.

The added effect of the tax system is the necessity of deciding what things, activities, or behaviors we are going to tax. One way of doing this is to provide a system of taxes for special uses—those who use or need the service help pay for it to a greater extent than those who do not. Other uses of taxes provide for the long-term good of the entire society as a whole and should be equally shared by all together.

The question is which is which? Is education just an advantage for those who use it, or is it for the vitality and productiveness of the entire economic and political system and for the health of the future community? Should those who have heavier, bigger vehicles pay more license tax because they are wearing out the road system faster than those with smaller or lighter vehicles? Should there be a luxury tax

A Practical Handbook for Moral Growth   86

that is different from a sales tax on food and clothes? If so, are some clothes "luxuries" and some not? How do we decide these issues?

6.7.3 Consequences of a Tax System

Clearly we all need to analyze these questions as logically as possible, thinking of as many of the consequences as we can. These are some suggestions I can imagine—no doubt you can imagine many others.

We should tax what we do not want, what is not desirable, or what is destructive.

- A gas tax or carbon tax should be high enough to reduce the use of fossil fuels, the reliance on foreign energy, and the pollution caused by burning carbon-based fuels.
- Cars and trucks should be taxed by size and weight to help recoup expenses for excessive wear and tear on the roads and to reduce long haul truck transportation and thereby encourage more local production.
- Pollution of all types should be taxed to prevent fouling our universally necessary clean air and clean water and to encourage responsible use of resources by manufacturing.
- Waste of all kinds should be taxed in order to prevent squandering resources, to encourage reuse and recycling of materials, and to reduce the accumulation of waste products.
- Potentially toxic materials should be highly taxed to prevent their waste and escape into the environment and to encourage alternate, safer materials.
- Houses and lots should be taxed on size in order to reduce sprawl.
- New materials should be taxed more than recycled and reused materials because new materials require more use of energy and potential pollution to acquire and result in more waste overall.
- Manufacturers should be required to "take back" products such as appliances, computers, or cars. that result in large amounts of

waste and toxic pollution in order to encourage design with reuse and recycling in mind.

We should reward or not tax what is desirable and healthy.

- Energy efficient cars, appliances, and manufacturing processes should be rewarded with tax credits or reduction of taxes compared to non-efficient products and methods.
- Clean processes and lack of waste (co-generation, manufacturing where one's waste is another's raw materials) should be rewarded with tax credits or reduction of taxes compared to polluting or wasteful processes.
- Deposits should be required for bottles and cans, thus providing rewards for their return so they are picked up and not thrown away and also leading to the increased value and reuse of what would be otherwise wasted.
- Local non-polluting and decentralized energy production should be encouraged with tax credits and ease of tying into the electric grid for resale.
- Education should be encouraged with tax credits and other incentives for "earning" educational funds through public service.

6.7.4 *Thought Experiment: Focusing on the System*
Choose some behavior or action you particularly want us to encourage or discourage.
Why do you think this?
How could it be accomplished?

7.0.0 Paths for the Nation

In a democracy we believe in a government of the people, by the people, and for the people. Yet sometimes affecting national policy seems hopeless. Decay is obvious because so much power and

A Practical Handbook for Moral Growth

wealth are in play. The system seems designed to work against moral Growth at every turn. The average citizen often is overwhelmed and overrun. For a democracy to function, moral Growth must overcome Decay in all areas of life, even at the national level. We need to be aware and think this through with both courage and determination. Then we need to act as individuals or groups to create a system that rewards moral Growth.

7.1.0 Swarm Theory

Swarm Theory concerns behaviors of animals in groups. Human beings are animals in groups, so maybe we can learn something from the observations that have lead to "swarm theory."

What are the characteristics of "swarm intelligence" that allow animals to respond together efficiently and effectively without a leader? How do colonies of ants, swarms of bees, schools of fish, flocks of birds, or herds of mammals function in normal life and in crisis whenever no one individual of the group is in charge? Their choices are self-organizing: no boss, no manager, no leader. According to research in animal behavior and in artificial intelligence, some basic rules emerge that may be just as applicable to human actions.

Patterning on bee-rules, first, humans need a diversity of options, then a free competition of ideas and recommendations or suggestions, and finally, a mechanism to narrow the choices gradually to a consensus. When people follow these rules, the process is to identify all the possibilities without being constrained by preconceptions or pressures to conform. The next step is to discuss the ideas completely enough so that the possibilities are clear and the best arguments have emerged. Last, a secret ballot or averaging or an auction method needs to be used to gather consensus. The trick for humans is to get a variety of independent-minded people who are willing to engage in give and take, to both speak and listen, before deciding.

According to Paul Miller, "Crowds tend to be wise only if individual members act responsibly and make their own decisions. A group won't be smart if its members imitate one another, slavishly follow fads, or wait for someone to tell them what to do. When a group is being intelligent, whether it's made up of ants or attorneys, it relies on its members to do their own part. For those of us who sometimes wonder if it's really worth recycling that extra bottle to lighten our impact on the planet, the bottom line is that our actions matter, even if we don't know how" (146-147). [Paul Miller. "Swarm Theory: Ants, Bees, and Birds Teach Us How to Cope with a Complex World." National Geographic July 2007:126-147.]

7.1.1   Being Collectively Smart

The keys to being collectively smart are, first, to decentralize control so that each of us is awake and can respond to whatever we personally see. "Local cues" are around each of us if we pay attention. Second, each individual must act responsibility and on his or her own initiative.

But smart human swarm behavior can be thwarted. Individuals may not act responsibly. They may not make their own decisions. They may imitate each other or be intimidated. They may wait for orders rather than deciding what is right because centralized control is so habitual. They may not base their choices on what they see, understand, and know from their local cues. But since no one sees everything or knows everything, each person must act on what is needed in his or her place. Act locally.

A Practical Handbook for Moral Growth   90

The question is how to train ourselves (and our children) to be independent-minded, rational and reasonable, observant, and responsible. It is easy to be intimidated, to be thoughtless or cynical, to ignore both our personal interest and the world beyond our small circle, and to let someone else do it. But that is Decay. It is easy, but it is death. How shall we choose life? We need to create a smart crowd that loves life, loves others, and is willing to take the risk of independence and freedom.

7.2.0   Realism and Growth or Decay

Is "real-politic" the only way to make choices or do we have another course? Reality is often defined in terms of money, power, greed, and fear. Look out for #1 and protect yourself first is the motto. This form of reality often works out as manipulating everyone else to one's own advantage, usually an immediate and short term advantage. Reality is using others for whatever they can give or we can take right now. Reality is playing our enemies off against each other, using our financial or physical power to bully our way, and saying whatever works. Does the one who yells the loudest always win? Should we be the authoritarian? The sadist? Is this is our only vision of reality?

Further, is the only alternate course naïve, rose-colored-glasses idealism? Should we let ourselves be taken advantage of, bullied by others, and filled with fear? Maybe we should choose to be sneaky, underhanded liars. Maybe we should just let others do any heavy lifting. Maybe we should use our golden tongues to say whatever seems to work for the moment and then conveniently forget or change our minds when the time comes to act. Do we have to choose the permissive or passive stance? Do we need to be masochists to survive?

7.2.1 Growth and Decay in Stories/Literature

Who shall we be and how shall we be are central questions for literature—the stories we tell to ourselves about ourselves show us who we are and who we might become. One of our most persistent themes is the question of whether Growth can actually "win" when Decay seems to hold all the power and wealth. Whether the story is The Lord of the Rings or Harry Potter or Star Wars, the question is central. Do we have to abandon Growth and go to the "Dark Side" because only raw power can win? For those who believe in moral Growth—in love, respect, freedom to choose, reason, individual responsibility, caring, and the common good—what are the possibilities? How can they win? What do they have to sacrifice to beat back Decay—the mind of iron, the love of death and dead materialism, the temptations of power and authoritarianism?

In these stories, everyone who believes in moral Growth must bear some burden. The young, small, and weak as well as the older or stronger or more experienced must contribute to the success of life over death. If any choose their own power or ignore the vitality and courage born of love, all will fall together. This universal story is a powerful one, and the temptations are common to all humans. Do we have a right to despair? Do we have hope? Can love prevail? Can we make a difference?

7.2.2 *Thought Experiment: Core Principles*

Do we as a nation have core principles that we will not abandon?

What do you think they are?

Why?

Does everyone agree?

How close can we come to a list that all would agree on?

7.2.3 "Authoritative" National Policy

An "authoritative" national policy stance would involve specific attitudes and behaviors:

- Real and engaged caring for and about others
- Making the limits of negative behavior known and following through with the natural consequences
- Using all the reason, logic, and appropriate negotiation we can muster with both our friends and our enemies
- Modeling for others how to make decisions and how to accept the efforts and the consequences that are required

7.2.4 *Thought Experiment:*
National Growth and Decay

Reconsider the lists of characteristics, causes, and effects of moral Growth and of moral Decay (2.1.0).

Why would any of them apply to nations?

How could either moral Growth or Decay be true of nations?

Are any of the attitudes and behaviors of Growth useful in the real world of global political and economic struggles?

Which ones would you recommend to the nation's leaders?

Why would you recommend them?

7.3.0 Economics

Separating the economic system or the market from the human mind and heart leads to moral Decay. Market economics plays a crucial role in our lives and needs to be thought through carefully. Human responsibility is a requirement for moral Growth, so corrupt economic systems are both the cause and the effect of moral Decay. How the risks and responsibilities for moral Growth within our economic systems are distributed and overseen is a central question.

7.3.1 Economic Systems

When we think of economic systems, we have many concerns about both the intended and unintended consequences of using resources, trading, and getting and spending money.

A communist system could certainly be based on the idealism of Biblical admonitions to share everything equally, to sell everything and give to the poor, to renounce earthly power, and to create a community of believers who hold everything in common. But Communism as it has actually worked out in our world has lead to extremes of power and control that have destroyed the very groups and economic classes whom it was ideally or theoretically supposed to protect. The temptations of total power come to all authoritarian systems, whether atheistic or theocratic, no matter how "pure" their philosophy—the more power, the more temptation, the more corruption. It is actually true that power corrupts—absolute power corrupts absolutely.

A democratic socialist system, while trying to prevent the temptations of authoritarianism, still falls into some of the same economic traps. Central planning by a few for the good of the masses yields narrow visions and paralyzing controls. In attempting to prevent abuses of power, it has often led to lack of vital creativity and abandonment of personal responsibility. When the authority to design life for virtually everyone falls into the hands of those who are fearful, small minded, or self-serving, then life is strangled or slowly starved. Maybe we need to revisit "swarm theory" again.

Capitalism is often said to be based on greed, fear, and manipulation. And it often is. Capitalism doesn't have to be predatory, but historically, so far at least, it has proven to be ruthless and thoughtless unless overseen by an alert public and by strong laws

A Practical Handbook for Moral Growth 94

to eliminate abuses of wealth and power. Often capitalists really believe that winning wealth means crushing everyone and everything other than themselves. People cease to be human and become machines for consumption, commodities to buy and sell in a marketplace where human needs, emotions, and intelligence are manipulated. People are objects to be "branded" for life. Predatory capitalists are ready and willing to use any means, any manipulation, any lie to get to the single bottom line of the greatest profit.

However, capitalism could mean a market full of variety and vitality where creativity and invention are rewarded. Education and personal care and attention could lead buyers to make wise choices and to make critical demands on the manufacturers, suppliers, and sellers. Capitalist power could come from millions of intelligent and thoughtful purchases. The people could have some control of the world they live in under capitalism—provided that they are willing to take their responsibilities seriously. The triple bottom line could include social justice and environmental responsibility as well as economic profit. Unfortunately, modern capitalism has so far worked extremely hard to create compliant masses—hungry, blind sheep willing to follow wherever they are led. Too often, modern consumers want only to feel like an accepted part of the flock, doing what the herder tells them to do and going where the herder wants them to go.

What is acceptable economic policy for the good of individuals, companies, and communities? What political policies and laws would create a fair and sustainable economic system?

7.3.2. *Thought Experiment: Priorities*

If you were the president of a company, what would be your personal priorities for the business?

If you were a worker in that company, what would be your personal priorities for the business?

If you were a shareholder in that company, what would be your personal priorities for the business?

If you were a customer of that company, what would be your personal priorities for the business?

Where are the conflicts?

What are the commonalities?

If the people who are in these roles believed that moral Growth was healthy for themselves, how would their priorities change?

If the people who are in these roles believed that moral Growth was healthy for their communities, how would their priorities change?

If the people who are in these roles believed that moral Growth was healthy for their nation, how would their priorities change?

If the people who are in these roles believed that moral Growth was healthy for their world and its natural systems, how would their priorities change?

Review the characteristics of Growth (2.1.0)—can they fit in an economic system?

7.4.0   Public Policy and the Common Good

Some actions and choices are beyond the resources, skills, or powers of individuals or local or state governments. In these cases the national government may need to organize or coordinate the projects that need to be done. In a representative democracy, we elect officials to stand in our stead, to represent us, in order to carry out these actions or make these decisions for the sake of all of us as a union. We contribute to these efforts through taxes that we levee on ourselves in order to accomplish our common goals.

7.4.1   *Thought Experiment:*
National Government Representing All Citizens
What responsibilities does the national government need to focus on for the sake of all of us together?

A Practical Handbook for Moral Growth   96

What necessary "chores" are required of the national government?
What national laws or policies would support the characteristics of Growth (2.1.0)
in our society?
What national laws or policies would encourage productive and dignified lives for all
citizens?
What should the national government oversee for the sake of all of us together?
For example, what do you think about these issues? Why would you choose specific
actions or support specific policies? How do the actions you chose encourage Growth?

- *Income to the public treasury from publicly owned land, leases, and resources*
- *Agricultural policies that oversee food safety*
- *Health laws and policies that oversee drug and health care efficacy*
- *Trade policies that require living wages and safe working conditions*
- *Energy or efficiency standards for vehicles, appliances, or housing*
- *Educational policy that measures student information and skills nationwide*
- *Environmental protection laws to require clean air and water nationwide*

7.5.0   Military

One of the required duties of the national government is to provide for the common defense. This leads us into a serious discussion of the reasons for and uses of a military system that includes a standing military, a reserve, and a national guard. These are critical concerns for any modern nation and its citizens.

7.5.1   War

Violence is not always caused by the love of death, and it is not necessarily a result of one group's fanatical leader worship. In fact, violence in defense of life is the reason most people accept killing and death—self-defense and the just war.

Defending life against the lovers of death and Decay may lead a nation to declare war. But if a leader misleads the fighters who are willing to defend life, then the use of the military in the service of life and moral Growth (the best reason for a volunteer military) is subverted and destroyed. The fighters who want to defend life are co-opted and their good intentions and sacrifices are turned into a service of Decay and death. Pretending that there is a threat when there is none has been used for political purposes for all of human history. It works to distract the citizens from real problems that the leader does not want them to notice. False threats force the nation to band together against an outsider and ignore problems within. A lie that misleads the citizens also might serve some other hidden motive that is not shared by the people themselves.

Vengeance is another possible reason for violence, but it is not in the service of present or future life. It is to "make up for" the past. If vengeance turns from legitimate self-defense into attacking an "enemy" that the leader has made into a scapegoat or one with whom the leader has a personal score to settle, then the border has been crossed. Crossing into Decay means violence is done for its own sake or for the wealth that it might bring to some. War as waged by the Japanese and Germans in World War II for conquest and power or to revenge old wrongs includes worship of the leader, masochistic sacrifice for the sacred land or country, and winning for the sake of power itself. This equates to the service of death because it is founded on a belief that my country exists and no other—extreme narcissism. The individual's dependence on the supreme leader or emperor or those in power goes far beyond any concrete sense of love or justice in objective reality.

A Practical Handbook for Moral Growth   98

7.5.2   The Enemy

When the enemy becomes the Other—vaguely evil and unreal, demonized into inhumanity—and when fear takes over, any of us can kill. In the absence of a real and present danger, unscrupulous or self-serving leaders incite fears, anxiety, and feelings of helplessness. Generally when the enemy becomes a real person, those extremes of violence are prevented or come into conflict with our feelings for others as humans like ourselves. Therefore, the Decayed leader tries to dehumanize an opponent to prevent his followers from seeing the enemy as real and specific persons. Or else we ourselves try to rationalize our need to kill, either in obedience or for a "larger" cause. The individual enemy becomes simply a representative of the bad leader or the bad ideology. The enemy is no longer a person at all.

7.5.3   Inhumanity

Some teachings deliberately create inhumanness in followers. Fanatic Islamists are often in this state, and there is no opening or time to counter the indoctrination of inhumanity. Suicide bombers, like kamikaze pilots, have been convinced that their deaths will make the world better, and in this way probably they believe that they are in the service of life. But more likely they have been convinced that they must avenge a past injustice or that their deaths are the will of God or the will of the exulted leader, certainly a service of death. Whose fault or credit is this?

The leader who sends others on the path of Decay is at fault, of course. But so are the followers who allow themselves to stop thinking and feeling. They stop reasoning, follow blindly, and are tempted to let others think for them. They give up personal responsibility. Of course, it is easy to see the power of the leader, but we have to accept the power of the follower as well. No leader goes into battle alone, and many don't go into battle at all. The follower can turn back from moral Decay if he or she accepts the reality of personal responsibility.

7.5.4 American Military

The American military are trained to be expert killers, but their training always emphasizes service of life and family as well as country. They represent a country that at its best sees itself as a leader for freedom, prosperity, and equality. Their training emphasizes sacrifice for these good ideals. The American military is trained to sacrifice in the service of life and against those who serve death. When the military is commanded to act in ways that serve death or Decay, the conflict becomes unbearable—loyalty is transferred to the small group, fighting for "my buddies," each one defending himself or herself in order to get back to "the real world," to "life."

In the Vietnam Conflict, for example, the confusion of the leaders, their love of power or fear of the loss of power, became clear. Then the military, especially those who were drafted, often subverted the "plan." They saw they were not in a war to defend freedom, independence, justice, or equality. They did not imagine themselves serving life. They knew prosperity, if any, would go to the few. They knew that the enemy guerrillas who belonged to the country itself saw themselves as defending their own country. They saw that at least some of the leaders of their local "friends" were self-serving, greedy, cowardly, or weak. These conflicts put those who thought about it in an impossible position and rewarded those who didn't think about it or who concentrated only on themselves.

With the change to a professional military, rather than either universal service or a drafted military, most Americans separated themselves from the realities of danger and war that the military and

A Practical Handbook for Moral Growth   100

their families understand only too well. If leadership encourages and rewards this separation from reality, it creates both ignorance and dependence in the average citizen. Moral Decay means fear and anxiety are encouraged among the passive but dependent followers. Cynical leaders manipulate the followers to focus on blind revenge or vague unnamed fears. Of course, this works very well as long as the people can be discouraged from using their reason and productive powers. As long as the focus is on vengeance and not on doing anything specific or concrete for Growth, Decay increases. The people, trusting the leaders, allow themselves to be manipulated. The leaders might be focused on power and money. Or perhaps they cannot actually imagine what they could do to make a positive difference. Either way the citizens are lead into a cycle of violence, fear, and dependence.

Is America unusual in this? Of course not. This has happened again and again throughout history.

7.5.5   Decay as a Failure of Imagination

The question is whether this Decay is a purposeful encouragement of vague anxiety, fear, helplessness, ignorance, and irrational hate and vengeance. Sometimes it certainly is. Yet sometimes Decay may be a failure of imagination and thought. We cannot even think of or imagine what might lead to Growth. Moral Growth means strength based on love of life, love of others, and the courage to be independent. How can we learn to imagine this?

7.5.6   *Thought Experiment:*
Citizen Questions in an External Crisis

Pick a recent actual physical *political or humanitarian crisis anywhere in the world. This could be an external or internal war, a health crisis like AIDS, or a natural disaster like drought or famine or earthquake, for example.*
Using these questions, think through the scenario you picked.

- *Compared to past similar experiences, what questions should we ask about this conflict?*
- *Who or what is the real enemy?*
- *Why is this person or thing or group an enemy?*
- *Is someone leading the violence and destruction or making it worse? What is his or her real reason?*
- *What concrete action could be taken to prevent future destruction?*
- *What concrete action could be taken to change the enemy himself or itself?*
- *If the enemy is a person or group, what concrete action could be taken to separate the followers from their leader(s) so that the followers can make better choices?*
- *If the enemy is a person or group, what concrete action can be done to encourage love of life instead of love of death in the followers of the enemy?*
- *If the enemy is a person or group, what concrete action can be done to encourage understanding and love of others in the followers of the enemy, rather than keeping the focus on group worship of country or leader?*
- *What concrete action can be done to support independence and responsibility rather than dependence and fear?*
- *What is the first concrete action to take?*
     Defensively if the danger is real, clear, and present
     Offensively to serve life, love, responsibility, and individual freedom.
What are the concrete actions to avoid?
     Cowardice, if courage is needed in defense
     Foolish or rash actions that serve only death, power, or wealth

For future reference: What could we have asked earlier that we didn't ask?

These are hard questions for citizens to ask, but in a democracy the people are responsible for thinking and for acting. Growth requires love, care, respect, independence, and wise use of free choice. Self-examination is a demanding process. Following the leader is easier.

A Practical Handbook for Moral Growth 102

7.5.7 Thought Experiment:
Citizen Questions in an Internal Crisis

Try this experiment using the case of a crisis with a leader or group in power who advocates Decay: violence and death, hate, extreme self-focus, dependence and fear, and helplessness.

Pick a specific country that is struggling with this issue right now if possible and if you know enough about the situation.

Imagine yourself as a citizen of that country.

- *Who is leading us in the wrong direction?*
- *Why is he doing this?*
- *What concrete action could be taken to prevent further damage or error?*
- *What concrete action could be taken to change the leader himself?*
- *What concrete action could be taken to separate the followers from this leader who is making bad choices that lead us toward Decay?*
- *What can be done to encourage love of life instead of love of death in his followers?*
- *What can be done to encourage understanding and love of others in the followers rather than their focus on worship of the country or the leader?*
- *What can be done to support independence and responsibility in the followers rather than dependence and fear?*
- *What can be done to maintain Growth in ourselves even in the face of the threats of Decay?*
- *What is the first concrete action to take?*
- *What are the concrete actions to avoid?*

7.6.0   What Should We Export?

Both moral Growth and Decay are contagious. Remembering Fromm's description that both the love of life and the love of death are communicated "without words, explanations, and certainly without any preaching," we need to consider what we are communicating with

103   Living As Though There Is a Tomorrow

the atmosphere that radiates around us. What is in the tone of our
voices? What is in our gestures?

7.6.1 Defining Freedom, Choice, and Success

Perhaps there is a problem with our own definition of freedom
and choice. Do we think freedom is for self-indulgence? Does
freedom to choose mean a choice of what to buy? If that is what we
want to export, then we are exporting death: death of responsibility,
death of love of life, and death of personal productive strengths.
Others don't want this version of Decay and death focused on self,
power, and money—we don't even want it, really.

De Tocqueville analyzed the conditions that lead to American
democracy in the early 1800s as America began its life as a nation. He
saw an entirely natural conflict between interest in our personal money
and power as opposed to our concern for community, the common
good, and independence. Americans have been willing to sacrifice for
both of these ideals. We understand that the common good and
independence are vital. At the same time we also naturally consider
our immediate comfort and needs for success as a long term goal. The
question is what is success? The test comes when the goal gets close:
Would I destroy my neighbor to get his field? Should I start a saloon
for money or a school for the future good—both? Would I use my
powers of persuasion to dominate and manipulate others for my own
advantage or to encourage independent thought and responsible self-
governance? There is always a potential conflict as humans set up their
societies and invent their traditions. Americans invented themselves
based on a Western religious and humanist value system, but within
that the tensions are strong.

7.6.2 *Thought Experiment: Tensions in Values*
How would we decide between these tensions?

A Practical Handbook for Moral Growth

Why would we decide to emphasize one way of acting or another?

When is the tension the greatest?

What is success and what is failure?

- *If success is individual and personal—what do I owe my neighbor?*
- *If what is mine belongs to me—what do I give away or give back to the community?*
- *What people or things outside of myself contributed to my success or failure?*
- *How did the community, the sacrifices of past citizens for the common good, help make my success possible?*
- *If the common good helps all of us together—how do I see to it that I get my share?*
- *If independent, educated thought is valuable—how should I control those who do not think as I do?*
- *If brains and rationality are key—what do I say to the person who seems irrational or incompetent?*
- *If true emotion and a good heart are central—what do I do with the person who seems to have no feelings or no social conscience?*
- *If I love my neighbor as myself—how do I keep my neighbor from taking advantage of me?*
- *If it is true that we should help the helpless ("even as you do this to the least of these, you do it to me," according to Jesus)—what do we do with the wastrel, the drunk, the crook, the lazy?*
- *If God helps those who help themselves—should I let others suffer in their own problems as an example or a punishment?*
- *If I am God's hands to help others—how should I teach them to help themselves?*

7.7.0   Foreign Policy

What is the purpose of our foreign policy? Does this seem like a ridiculous question? What are we doing in the world and why? Often leaders or professional experts have precise answers to this, but citizens are imagining some entirely different purpose for those choices. Because we do not discuss this honestly, all of us, both experts and citizens, are often shocked, amazed, chagrinned, even afraid of the results of our own behaviors.

7.7.1   Policies Leading to Decay

· If our policy is based on Decay, primarily on short term advantage, immediate power, and the generation of wealth for ourselves, then we are often sucked into discrimination against the very people our democratic or humanitarian principles would normally support.   On the one hand, perhaps our policy is nakedly and purposefully based on Decay, and we are just not admitting it to ourselves. When we act on principles of Decay, we find ourselves in violent power conflicts of tribalism and class.   We are lost in false patriotism that hides the truth of our own actions from us.   The promotion of personal power and wealth becomes entangled with national priorities, dragging all of us into a swamp.   We cannot extricate ourselves from this swamp without facing an intense national crisis, soul searching, embarrassment, and even humiliation.   We are ashamed because we know that we have been caught in a conflict or power play when we should have known better.   We recognize we should have chosen more wisely.   But the Decaying power of the tribe or the fatherland or blind patriotism or raw violence has overthrown the principle of Growth.

On the other hand, our policy could be based on promoting long term good both for ourselves and others.   Then would support individual productivity and dignity for all.   We would encourage local responsibility and leadership for Growth.   But we would ask different questions and use different priorities in deciding on our policies.   The principles of Growth would probably change our

A Practical Handbook for Moral Growth   106

choices and behaviors in significant ways.   They probably would change our choice of friends and enemies and would change our use of foreign aid.

7.7.2   Thought Experiment: Imagining Foreign Aid

Where do you imagine our foreign aid goes?
What is our nation's definition of "aid"?
Is it cash or raw materials or manufactured goods or services?
What would the difference be among these kinds of aid?
Who do you imagine receives aid when it is sent somewhere?
How do you imagine the receiver uses our aid within his or her country?
Do you think this is monitored in some way?
Do some research to find out what really happens to our foreign aid in a place you are interested in.

7.7.3   Thought Experiment: Designing a Foreign Aid System

From your perspective, how should we spend our foreign aid dollars?
If you were designing or voting on foreign aid expenditures, how would you design the system? What would your priorities be since there are bound to be limits to how much aid is available?
Make an actual list of what your priorities are from the perspective of our own nation.
If we give foreign aid, should we expect something in return?
What should we expect as a result of our aid?
Why should we expect something in return or expect some specific result from giving aid?
How is foreign aid a tool for reward and punishment?
Should all foreign aid be based on reward and punishment?

7.7.4   Foreign Aid for Growth

Based on the principle of Growth, I would argue that the best use of foreign aid is to promote and encourage the characteristics of

Living As Though There Is a Tomorrow

Growth: attraction to and love of life, love of others moving from self to neighbors, strangers, and nature or all living things, and a willingness to risk independence and freedom. If we ask whether our gifts are going to create the characteristics of Growth perhaps we can make wiser choices for the long term good. We can promote a healthier world and ethically stronger and more productive people everywhere.

How can our gifts create Growth?

- independence
- individual productive activity
- economic sufficiency
- mental/psychological abundance
- reason
- objectivity
- rational judgments and critical thinking
- awareness of reality
- acceptance of truths that are valid for all peoples
- orientation to the present and future while understanding the past
- integrated and united personalities
- structural and intellectual growth
- love for processes of life that involve both feeling and thinking
- service to and defense of life
- reverence for an enlarged circle of life
- joy and gladness
- warm and affectionate contacts with others
- freedom
- lack of threats
- inner harmony and strength
- stimulating and interesting life
- equal justice for all
- dignified lives without fear and anxiety
- freedom to be active and responsible in society

A Practical Handbook for Moral Growth

108

- basic security
- original and adventurous intelligence and character
- an awareness of the self as a complete human
- a concern for the common good
- acceptance of useful tasks and equity in doing them
- acceptance of the risks and power of responsible choices
- helpfulness
- understanding of realistic alternatives and consequences
- imagination of the possibilities for good
- willingness to struggle with the frustrations and burdens of humanness
- fortitude
- insight
- self-confidence
- integrity
- courage

7.7.5 Suggestions for Foreign Aid

Aid in education and health care is the most valuable for promoting and encouraging Growth. This aid needs to encourage independence, personal productivity, a wise attention to long term consequences of actions, and a desire for a dignified life of freedom and personal responsibility. Women and children, not just men, and ordinary citizens, not just leaders, need to be considered and targeted in giving aid. The principles of Growth can be taught and modeled if we choose to do so.

My list would include these forms of aid. What would your list include?

- Money and leadership aid should facilitate education, especially for women and children. This should include teachers' colleges that can lead to immediate and long-term social growth. Aid should be given first for universal elementary education and to educate local teachers so that local leadership and responsibility can begin as soon as possible. It is absolutely essential that both girls and boys be required to have equal access to education. Building schools out of local materials with local labor and providing teacher training are important concrete actions. A society with free, educated, and responsible women is inevitably safer, healthier, and more productive than one where women and girls are ignored or oppressed.

- Aid for basic health care should go to teaching hospitals to train local nurses and doctors, to local clinics, and to free birth control. These are crucial to promoting safety, local responsibility, and dignity. This type of aid reduces anxiety and dependence and promotes willingness to look to the future with courage and confidence.

- Aid needs to provide for a local sense of self-sufficiency and useful care taking. This means facilitating safe water supplies and basic sanitation, sustainable and organic agriculture, local markets and trade, self-governance, and a dignified life under a local system of fair laws and equal justice. Education for local control and maintenance is necessary. Imposing an alien industrialized, potentially toxic system of agriculture and trade for our own gain is deadly.

- It is increasingly obvious that local energy production is essential. Small-scale wind, roof-top solar, farmyard bio-digesters, or ethanol from waste must be matched to local technical education and mechanical skills so that citizens can personally maintain and

A Practical Handbook for Moral Growth 110

eventually invent appropriate energy production. Independence and local productive living is the key result.

- Any aid must result in freedom and self-determination for both women and men. Local citizens need support in understanding their real choices and in exerting their own will and effort. Any aid which creates dependence on outside mechanisms and authoritarian leaders, which reduces local control of productivity, or which prevents free choices or personal responsibility cannot result in moral Growth.

7.7.6 Threats to Moral Growth

International standards for the use of money for the common good in order to promote a safe and healthy environment, equal justice, and education need to be openly discussed among donors. This would reduce the perception of threat or anxiety in "competing powers." But we do need to understand that education for both girls and boys, local independent productivity and responsibility, courage, and freedom to make choices are threats to moral Decay. Those who are interested in personal power and greed, wherever they may be, will find these forms of Growth to be a threat to their own self-interest and will often use deception or violence to try to beat them down. Growth needs to be defended with courage.

7.7.7 Dangers of Decay in Foreign Aid

I would argue that foreign aid should not be used to promote or encourage moral Decay. This means it should avoid all attraction to or love of death or violence, extreme self-love, and dependence and fear. If we ask whether our gifts are going to promote, encourage, or facilitate Decay, maybe we can make wiser choices for the long term.

Maybe we can help to prevent the destruction, anger, violence, and hate that would otherwise be inevitable.

How can we prevent our gifts from leading to moral Decay?
- dependence
- incompetence
- impotence
- economic scarcity
- mental/psychological poverty
- irrational or uncritical thought
- fanaticism
- an assumption that truth is valid only for one group
- orientation to the past to revenge old wrongs
- cults of personality or leader worship
- weakness
- anxiety
- stagnation
- passivity
- love of or fascination with death and mechanism
- addiction to thrills or excitement
- actions for evil
- despair
- cynicism
- fright
- emptiness
- emphasis on control of others
- injustice
- inequality
- seeing others as inhuman or inferior
- unquestioning obedience
- willingness to do harm
- exploitation of others
- passivity

A Practical Handbook for Moral Growth

- unwillingness to struggle with frustrations of humanness
- lack of insight
- cowardice
- personal moral or ethical paralysis

7.7.8 Suggestions for Avoiding Decay in Foreign Aid

Foreign aid that supports or encourages moral Decay includes some specific dangers. But there are equally specific ways to avoid the dangers of Decay.

- Behaviors based on the principles of moral Decay cannot be rewarded in any way. Decay will certainly lead to authoritarian power and personal wealth. But while this may appear to create a "stable" society, it is virtually always a result of the love and promotion of death and violence, discrimination against anyone who is not in the power structure, and a willingness to destroy the productivity and health of the Earth. When we give aid to those who would reward dependency, fear, threat, a cult of personality, or narrow violent tribalism, we are condemning our children to suffer for our short-sightedness and greed. We are also promoting the social disintegration of those we are pretending to help.

- No aid should be given to corrupt, selfish leaders and bureaucrats, neither to siphon off for themselves nor to reward their followers and punish their opponents within their countries. When aid goes to those who misuse it, even the best charitable intentions are crippled.

- No money should be used for weapons and violence. Even though we have weapons manufacturers who are eager and willing to supply these forms of manufactured aid, they inevitably lead to an escalation of posturing, threat, and violence. There is no reason to facilitate Decay in this way. Often we hear arguments that these forms of aid are for defense. While this is no doubt sometimes true, it rarely works out in the end, and it supports and encourages all forms of violence, including violence by authoritarian leaders against the citizens themselves. Any weapons for defense must be closely monitored and controlled.

- Any time that corruption is uncovered, aid should be withdrawn from that leader or bureaucracy in order to remove the temptation of Decay and to reduce or eliminate the source of corrupt power. Coordination of investigations with non-governmental organizations, independent religious or charity groups, or impartial observers can help find out the level of efficiency and fairness inside the system. Any provider of aid who only knows those in power is bound to fail.

- A requirement of aid must be justice and equality for all, including gender equity. Any form of aid that goes to an "old-boys" power group will inevitably lead to moral Decay, unless it is intensively monitored. Aid needs to reward personal and local responsibility because those who would enforce their power by threat of ethnic or gender discrimination cannot lead a society to become safe, healthy, productive, free, and responsible.

7.7.9 *Thought Experiment: Walking in Another's Shoes*

Put yourself in another's shoes.

Pretend the country where you lived was receiving aid from another country. After Hurricane Katrina in 2005 foreign countries offered America aid. Perhaps this can help you imagine what foreign aid would be like?

How would you want foreign aid money to be spent?

If the aid were in the form of manufactured goods or food, how should it be distributed?

What would be your list of prioritized needs for aid based on your understanding of the good of your place or country as a whole?

Who should receive and disburse aid money, food, or goods?

Who should decide what the rules are for using it?

What are the responsibilities of the "giver"?

What are the responsibilities of the "receiver"? .

8.0.0   Social Choices and Consequences

8.1.0   Defining Consequences

Questions about the short-term and the long-term results of our decisions and actions are commonplace. We have always asked about gains and losses in any question of competing choices. We have always considered the cost-benefit analysis. What we haven't asked is what is "winning" and what is "losing"—what do these words mean to us? Who or what wins? Who or what loses? Who gains? Who is harmed? What is gained? What is lost?

One of the most striking results of discussions on this topic happened in England at an Oxford Round Table. At the beginning of my presentation on sustainable environmental and humanitarian ethics and before any explanation had been offered, I asked the participants to circle the characteristics of Growth from a list of descriptive words. Assuming that this meant "Economic or Political Growth," one of the participants later said that he began circling descriptions like irrational or uncritical thought, exploitation of others, injustice, inequality, cynicism, good only for the self and personal group, manipulation of others. As soon as the word "ethical" or "moral" was added to "Growth"—all of the answers changed to the opposite: critical thought processes and reason, acceptance of useful tasks and equity, joy and gladness, equal justice, freedom to be active and responsible in society, affectionate contacts with others, inner harmony and strength, creativity, independence.

Why would this happen? Clearly there is an intense and complex reaction to these issues. "Growth" is a word loaded with conflicting baggage. We need to consciously examine our language and definitions in our everyday lives and choices. We need to closely examine what we mean and how our thoughts are working, or not working, in the real world. Also, we need to do this as individuals, as social and cultural groups and communities, and as citizens at all levels.

We need to ask these questions in terms of the principles of moral Growth and moral Decay because Decay is so attractive to our society's cultural values in many significant ways. We strongly value power and wealth. Often we see altruism, kindness, generosity, and love as wimpy and weak, unless they lead to some measurable gain for us. Both our business analysis and too often our judgment of education tell us that all worthwhile things are measurable and quantifiable. Our religious ethic has many times argued that wealth and power are signs of God's favor. While "Social Darwinism" (survival of the fittest in the social struggle) may feel morally wrong to us when or if we think of it, we truly assume that it must be right. The social winners will naturally be the fittest and the best. The winners will be the most physically beautiful, the richest, the most powerful, the most celebrated, the most witty and charming. The result of this natural attraction is that Decay is hard to resist and hard to argue against. Often we do not see the characteristics of moral Growth as signs of the fittest and best in our society. In doing this we condemn ourselves to choosing death.

8.1.1   Rational and Practical vs. Irrational and Impractical

What is rational or practical for us depends on how we have been guided by our personal observations. This includes our experiences and immersion in our personal and social cultures.

Moral Decay can appear rational and practical, at least for us personally and for the short term:

- Rational and practical choices often encourage looking out for "number one" and so are either self-centered or focused on the advantage of a small, select group.
- Rational and practical choices are often based on immediate personal or group gain.
- Rational and practical choices are often intended to increase personal or select group power, so the ends naturally justify the means.

Moral Growth can appear irrational and impractical:

- Choices that are "other"-centered and focused on the good of the greater community or for the sake of long-term consequences or future life may seem irrational or impractical.
- Not getting an obvious or immediate pay back seems irrational or impractical.
- Being altruistic or not gaining personal or select-group advantage appears irrational and impractical, certainly in the short term.

8.1.2   Creating Our World by Choice

Because of these facts of life, we often choose behavior or attitudes that promote Decay because they help us or our personal select-group win an advantage. Whether choices are for individualistic, select-group, or authoritarian purposes, Decay can result from what seem to be practical choices. So why should we choose moral Growth?

Thinking back over the list of characteristics of people and societies choosing Decay or choosing Growth (2.1.0), which person would you want to be? Which **society** would you want to live in? What kind of world do you want your children and grandchildren and great-grandchildren to inherit? We create this world everyday with every choice.

The basic definitions of Decay and Growth are these:
Moral Decay is characterized by
- An attraction to or love of death, force, violence, mechanism, and power and their processes
- Extreme self-love, self-focus, and absolutism
- Parasitic dependence, fear, and authoritarianism

Moral Growth is characterized by
- An attraction to or love of life and its processes
- Love of others that moves out from the self to neighbors, strangers, and nature or all living things (even to the land, air, and waters)
- A willingness to risk action based on independence, freedom, responsibility, and personal choice

8.1.3   Actual Choices

Some of our actual choices can illustrate the power and logic of Decay as we live it.

In the protection of New Orleans, we chose to tightly constrict the river with levees, allowing for no "worthless" floodplains. We chose to create shipping channels that tore up the swamps and marshes and funneled the dangerous storm surges into the city. We chose to cut down the forests and cypress groves for immediate gain. We chose to dismantle the vegetation on barrier islands. We chose to

A Practical Handbook for Moral Growth

build many neighborhoods well below sea level. Why? Because we truly believed in the power and invincibility of our machines. We believed that our wealth producing processes demanded it. Especially, we believed in our ability to outsmart and conquer nature. The natural protections were destroyed. We had no respect for the diverse systems that actually worked. We didn't want to know why they worked or how we could cooperate with them. Our answer was short term, violent, dependent on machines, and centered only on our immediate desires to create wealth and power. We were left vulnerable and helpless in the end.

We create cities filled with green lawns, golf courses, and swimming pools in the desert. We pump antique waters out of the aquifers to flush a million toilets and to spray into the air in coordinated fountain, light, and music shows. We race over the fragile soils, tearing up the ground and muddying the few water holes for "fun." Our hotels rise into the sky, but we never think to wonder what happened to the gorgeous hanging gardens of Babylon.

We want cheap fish, so we vacuum everything out of the sea. We throw back the "worthless" dead by-catch, keeping the quarterly profit to pay the executives, the shareholders, and the loans for even more enormous factory ships to win the competition to suck out the last fish. We hang death nets for miles. We plow up the seabed to either catch or destroy every living thing. We battle for the right to kill the last remnants. Meanwhile, we fight against marine reserves that might help replenish a little of the legendary richness of the sea. Complete harvesting of resources for today is judged more important than sanctuaries for future reproduction.

We want cheap oil for our petroleum culture, so we wage wars. We want cheap energy so we subsidize nuclear power plants whose waste will be toxic for tens of thousands of years, if it isn't made into nuclear weapons first. We reward centralized, highly vulnerable systems in every way politically possible. We don't want a village windmill or solar cells on every roof top or a manure digester in every farmyard or garbage-dump methane to create our energy. And we certainly don't want efficient transportation—because it is not profitable enough today. Choosing for today only, we ignore the lessons of the past and the hopes of the future.

We want cheap chicken, beef, and pork, so we create factory farms and drive the integrated, sustainable farmer out of business. Special subsidies are handed out to corporate investors and absentee landlords. Special rules allow lakes of manure and acres of animals packed together. Special corporate protections prevent consumers from knowing where their meat comes from, whether the workers were paid a fair wage and worked in safe conditions, or whether they are eating growth hormones and antibiotics. The growth of super profit today is more critical than the super-bugs of tomorrow.

8.1.4   Choosing our Relationship to Nature

It is never possible to do just one thing. All things are interconnected—the humans, the animals, the plants, the air, the water, the land itself. The questions of moral Growth or moral Decay include our relationship to Nature.

As Aldo Leopold states in "The Land Ethic," "No important change in ethics was ever accomplished without an internal change in our intellectual emphasis, loyalties, affections, and convictions." We need to use our reason, our sense of duty, our love of life, and our deepest beliefs to choose moral Growth in our interdependency with natural systems of all kinds. Otherwise we will destroy ourselves.

Our reason includes knowing as well as interpreting the meaning of what we know. We know that nothing in the natural world is linear. All of nature's atoms, molecules, organic and inorganic are part of the cycles of life. We know that in nature there is no waste. We know that only man-made atoms and molecules do not fit into the perpetually revolving circles of life. How should we interpret this?

In the 1980s Barry Commoner came to speak at the Minnesota college where I teach. His Four Laws of Ecology from The Closing Circle are justly famous: 1. Everything is connected to everything else; 2. Everything must go somewhere; 3. Nature knows best; and 4. There is no such thing as a free lunch. In that speech he added a fifth law: If we don't add something, it isn't there.

His argument has been taken up by architect William McDonough and chemist Michael Braungart in Cradle to Cradle: Remaking How We Make Things (2002). They add a technical circle as well as the biological circle and then contend that with proper design humans have the ability to remove the waste and deadly toxins that will never fit into a healthy world: "Poor design [...] reaches far beyond our own life span. It perpetuates what we call *intergenerational remote tyranny*—our tyranny over future generations through the effects of our actions today" (43). If we recognize this influence and our responsibility for it, we will live as though there is a tomorrow.

"We grieve only for what we know" [Aldo Leopold, "July"]. We know—do we grieve? Do we feel anything? Can we use both our heads and our hearts?

One direction this leads is the question of duty. Once we have facts and understand their meaning, how shall we apply them? What do the facts and interpretations mean to us? What does it mean to be dependent on the processes of life? Do we have a duty to stop doing harm to ourselves? More important perhaps, do we have a duty to stop sending the tyranny of our harmful choices out into the future?

This then leads us to love and what E.O. Wilson calls biophilia, the love of life. We do usually love ourselves and our group, our children and our grandchildren. We do sometimes love other humans, both neighbors and strangers. But do we love life? The processes of life are complex and diverse, often chaotic, even uncontrollable. Can we find it in ourselves to love life?

Our natural tendency is to prefer stability and control so much that we are willing to use any amount of power, any mechanism or force, any violence to defend ourselves against nature's constant motion. This is for good reason because over millennia humans have struggled to survive and thrive. "Nature" has sometimes seemed to be not only our great benefactor, our Mother Earth, but also our worst enemy. The chaos of living needed to be conquered, defeated, controlled, or smothered for the sake of the future. But now our powers of death are so great that we are straining at the circles of life itself. It appears that we would rather die in the collapse than have peace. Loving life is hard for us on many levels.

We need to decide what we believe about this. If we do finally break the circles of life and interdependency, what will our future become? Will our stewardship be found wanting because the house is in ruins? Believing that we have the freedom and responsibility to choose moral Growth rather than moral Decay puts a heavy burden on us. It is easier to be passive, awaiting the fate that someone else will construct for us. It is also tempting to fall back on our passion for power and self-will.

Creating the future by choice using our reason, duty, love, and belief is possible. We have minds for reason, for knowing, and for

A Practical Handbook for Moral Growth   122

interpreting. We have hearts to apply our duty and love. We have spirits and energy for belief. Do we have the courage to choose life?

8.1.5   Questioning for the Common Good

Questions can lead us to discover the realities of our choices. Here is one set that can be applied to many choices:

- What are the possible and/or likely good consequences of the action, law, or product in question?
  What is the degree of benefit?
  Who or what benefits?

- What are the possible and/or likely harmful consequences of the action, law, or product?
  What is the degree of harm?
  Who or what is harmed?

- How much study or thought has gone into this plan or action?
  Who has done the work?
  Do I trust the quality of the work?
  Do I trust the motives behind the plan or action?

- Is there a difference between the short term effects and the long term effects?
  If there is, is the short term or the long term more important?
  Why and to whom is the short term or the long term important?

- Are the benefits worth the potential risks to the world, to society, to individual others, to me?

> [based on Sheldon Rampton and John Stauber,
> Trust Us, We're Experts (2001)]

8.1.6   *Thought Experiment: What is the Common Good?*

Pick a recent public health or environmental issue and consider these questions:
What is the public good in this case?

Is this the same as the common good?
What would you consider to be the worse/worst choice?
What is a better choice?
How can you recognize the best choice?

8.1.7 Choosing a Path toward Moral Growth

If we went back to the causes and effects of Decay, we would see the signs of the road we are on. Do we all really want to go where we are headed? Do we love violent "solutions" of power and machines that much? Do we want to provide special privileges for the small groups who are friends of those in power? Do we want to be constantly dependent on giant, centralized systems of monocultures, feedlots, factory farms and factory ships, long petroleum supply chains, nuclear power production manipulated by corrupt traders, and mountains full of toxic waste? Are we so passive that we need industrial-strength entertainment because we can't play or sing or dance for ourselves anymore? Do we really want to lead the whole world down this path?

If we wanted to go on a different road, one with signs of moral Growth along the way, where would we aim? Do we have enough strength, courage, or joy to love life? Can we care about anything or anyone other than ourselves? Are we willing to take the risks necessary to create independent lives of freedom? Can we make choices that result from both thought and care? True, this is a harder way. It puts more responsibility on each of us to do the thinking and the caring. But the path of moral Growth is a healthier and wiser way to go—for ourselves, for our children, for our great-grandchildren—also for our neighbors near and far—and for the natural world. This path leads toward more imaginative humanitarian and environmental ethics.

A Practical Handbook for Moral Growth 124

We can deliberately choose a path toward moral Growth. We don't need to make ourselves or other nations, people, or businesses dependent, passive, and self-centered. We can work with the natural systems instead of against them, learning from nature's diverse complexities, built-in redundancies, and myriad interrelationships, instead of creating simplified and centralized uniformity. We can aim for education that empowers people—girls and boys, men and women—to be independent, creative, reasonable, thoughtful, and caring. We can provide aid to others and a tax system that encourages independence, responsibility, and self-control. We can choose to voluntarily limit our destruction of everything around us. We can be both human and humane, not cogs in the wheels of a machine.

8.2.0   Contagion and Inoculation

The atmosphere we produce as individuals or groups is contagious. Our tone of voice and gestures send messages even though we are perhaps unaware of them. So we need to consider how we are affecting others for better or worse. Are we spreading Decay or spreading Growth?

An inoculation uses a dead or disabled piece of the virus it is fighting against to produce a reaction in the body that will fight off future infections. Moral Decay can inoculate us so we will not "catch" Growth—but moral Growth can also inoculate us so that we will not accept Decay.

8.2.1   Inoculation against Moral Growth is Easy

<u>**Growth needs to be whole**</u>. When Decay tries to inoculate us against Growth, it takes a piece of the idea of Growth, then kills or disables it, and injects it into our conscious or unconscious thoughts to prevent us from choosing Growth. Decay can cause Growth to rot at

any weak spot. "Responsibility is so boring—it's no fun at all." "Love is too mushy and gluey; it holds you down—it holds you back—it prevents you from doing what you want to do." "You have to choose to care about either humans or nature—you can't care about both— you have to choose either the economy or ecology." "Real independence and freedom mean not having to care about others." "Freedom and choice are dangerous; it's better to just do as I tell you—then you won't have anything to worry about."

8.2.2 Disabling Moral Growth Piece by Piece

<u>Growth needs to be whole</u>, so Decay can also remove parts of the idea of Growth in order to stunt or disable it. Men have often told women, "I love you so much that I want to protect you from danger, to keep you from worry and the trouble of making hard decisions. Women are so fragile and emotional that it is really better to let me take care of everything and do all the thinking. You might make a wrong choice. You're really not capable of understanding important matters like money, religion, law, and politics. I'll tell you whom to vote for. I'll tell you what to believe about God. I'll tell you what to do with your body. I'll let you know when I want to discuss something that might interest you. Don't worry your pretty little head about anything. Here's some money so you can go shopping."

In similar ways other stereotypes also remove pieces of moral Growth and twist them, pretending to be good, but really producing rot:

- Slaves/women/children are helpless—they can't cope with the independence and choices of freedom and risks of responsibility—they need someone to tell them what to think and do.
- I love my husband, but he is such a baby.

A Practical Handbook for Moral Growth 126

- She certainly loves life—even though all she thinks about is herself and what she wants—she creates excitement everywhere she goes.
- He can't do anything right—the way I want it done.
- Love 'em and leave 'em—that's the way to avoid getting caught in the commitment trap.
- She likes getting beaten up—she asks for it.
- He likes me to be weak and helpless—I let him pretend to be strong.
- As long as the children have friends and fun, they don't notice the troubles at home.
- Children need to just be children—they shouldn't have to help or be respectful or be thankful—they're too young to worry about all that.
- My children belong to me, so I can do what I want with them.
- I would never spank my kids—yelling is okay because words will never hurt them.
- I pretend I'm listening to him to make him happy, and then I just do whatever I want.

We can't choose a piece of moral Growth, like love of others, and throw away love of the processes of life with all their chaos and complexity. Love of others doesn't mean authoritarian control of them. Love of family doesn't mean taking away the freedom to make appropriate choices. Love of children doesn't mean protecting them from the steps they need to take to learn to be independent but also thoughtful of others at the same time. Love is not an excuse for creating fear and dependence nor for exercising controlling domination or violence. Independence is neither an excuse for self-centeredness nor for mindless rebellions. **Moral Growth needs to be whole.**

8.2.3 Inoculation against Decay is Planted by Example

But moral Growth is not helpless. Growth can inoculate against Decay by planting seeds. It sheds seeds that spread far and wide, sometimes lying dormant waiting for the opportunity to sprout. Examples of joyful interaction with life are seeds of Growth. Examples of love of others and love of nature are seeds of Growth. Examples of independent thinking, wise choices, and willingness to make the effort and endure the frustrations of trying and risking are seeds of Growth. These seeds come from others who surround us with examples of Growth. An atmosphere of confidence, courage, graciousness, and delight spreads around them. Their gestures of love, acceptance, and encouragement communicate louder than words. Their words of wisdom linger on long after they themselves are gone:

Friendship is "the promotion of the other's good for the other's own sake." Aristotle

"The Fruit of the Spirit is love, joy, peace, patience, kindness, goodness, faithfulness, gentleness, and self control."
Galatians 5: 22-23

"Let the beauty we love be what we do.
There are hundreds of ways to kneel and kiss the ground." Rumi

"In our every deliberation, we must consider the impact of our decisions on the next seven generations."
Great Law of the Haudenosaunee [Iroquois]

8.3.0 Innocence and Experience

We each journey from innocence to experience. On this journey we all gradually discover how to relate to the world around us,

A Practical Handbook for Moral Growth 128

both human and natural. We take this journey in our families and our governments, in our businesses and our institutions. We all grow and change through our observations, experiences, and traditions—even through our thoughts and experiences during this very minute. We decide day by day through each action and choice what will come to be important, valuable, true, and right for us. Innocence has little to do with age, but much to do with circumstances. Innocence may not necessarily be positive. Experience does not necessarily create Decay.

8.3.1 Positive and Negative Innocence

We can observe and describe positive innocence. Innocence can be the traits that we love and admire in children and those who are childlike. Innocence can be fearless, loving, accepting, optimistic, trusting, spontaneous, believing in absolute justice, taking joy in small things. On the other hand, we can also describe innocence in negative terms: childish, naïve, self-centered, afraid of the bogyman under the bed, immature, lacking in perspective, simplistic, and having a short attention span. These descriptions could apply to children, but not necessarily. For good or ill, adults can be innocent, too.

8.3.2 Negative and Positive Experience

We all have seen enough "experience" in dysfunctional families, cruel and totalitarian governments, dishonest but powerful corporations, and manipulative or cowardly institutions to realize that experience can be ugly. Terrible experiences are only too real. Experience is no respecter of age, and sometimes falls heavily upon those who are far too young. Terrible experiences can create extreme negativity. Overwhelmed by fears and lack of trust, those who are experienced often use clichés like "so what," "who cares," or "boring" to hide their anxieties. The experienced can become jaded, hard-boiled, suspicious, hopeless, cynical, believing there is no justice or right. And if there are such things as justice and right, then creating them and holding on to them are too hard. This is moral Decay. It spreads to us not only by our personal experiences but also by the atmosphere, tone, and gestures in our families, governments, businesses, or institutions, in all we see at work around us.

But experience does not have to result in this negative world view. Experience can lead to Growth. It can lead to courage in the face of very real fears. The positive result of experience can be a realization that love and justice, which seem so difficult or even impossible, are still worth the effort. With experience we can recognize and accept the complexity and ambiguity of life, constructive caring for others, and the ability to focus and concentrate energy for the tasks at hand.

8.3.3   Growth as Positive Experience

When we examine the description of ethical Growth, what we see is a positive version of experience: love of life and the processes of living, including its uncontrollable messiness and chaos; love of both other humans and nature in all their complexities; and a willingness to take the responsibility and risks of independence, freedom, and choice.

8.3.4   Growth as a Whole Unit

Growth must have all of these. Independence or freedom without love of others degrades into license and self-centeredness. Love of humans without love of nature is doomed to destructive failures and short sightedness, but love of nature without love of humans is self-defeating. Love of life without accepting its natural processes and the power of chaos devolves into either mechanical

A Practical Handbook for Moral Growth

force or loss of hope. Responsibility without love of life is self-destructive and controlling of others. **Decay can start by eating away at any vulnerable spot, creating rot and softness that can spread unnoticed. But Growth must come as a whole.**

Growth at its best and most effective is a ball—with a center that is mysterious and hidden and covered with complexities that appear as we circle around it, examining it from all perspectives. Of course, as humans our natural tendency is to cut this wholeness apart in order to choose whatever slice of Growth seems handy for our momentary need, but Growth is a sphere, not a straight line or a narrow slice. Love of life, love of others, including nature, and accepting the risk of independent thought and action are woven together in both humanitarian and environmental ethics and cannot be separated.

Missing any part of moral Growth means beginning the unraveling. Gradually we tend toward Decay. Decay seems so easy and so obvious, so practical and immediately effective, until we follow-the-leader off the edge into an abyss. Aldo Leopold warned us about this universal human tendency decades ago when he said, "By and large, our present problem is one of attitudes and implements. We are remodeling the Alhambra with a steam shovel and are proud of our yardage."

But he also challenged us in "The Land Ethic": "No important change in ethics was ever accomplished without an internal change in our intellectual emphasis, loyalties, affections, and convictions." If we want to choose Growth, we need to engage our brains and reason, our sense of duty, our love, and our beliefs. All must be present and active in each of us in order to accomplish a change in ethics toward moral Growth and away from moral Decay.

8.3.5 Growth as a Source of Ethics

Decay can be totalitarian, violent, and terrifying, but Decay can also lure us down an apparently easier, often imperceptibly downhill, road. On the other hand, Growth is so much more effective in the long term, so much healthier, so much more beautiful and joyful. Even though Growth is harder and demands constant education, thought, and care, it will lead us on an ethical path through life.

The creation of humanitarian and environmental ethics now and into the future depends on our personal willingness to be examples of Growth in our institutions, our governments, and our families. The atmosphere we create through our tones and gestures, our words and deeds, at work and at home, will be contagious, for good or ill. Through every choice, attitude, and action, big and small, we can choose moral Growth for the sake of both the human and natural world.

A Practical Handbook for Moral Growth

FUTURE THOUGHTS

9.0.0 Discovery of Choices and Consequences for the Future

Each of us individually and all of us together need to embark on a voyage of discovery into our heads and hearts. What is it that matters? What do we truly care about? Whom do we consider in making our choices? What rationalizations or excuses strongly influence us? What do we believe? What do we think? Where does our duty lie? What do we love? How should we act? How should we choose?

9.1.0 *Thought Experiment, continuing into the future: Personal Discoveries*

What do you think?
What do you feel?
What do you believe?
What do you choose?
How do you act?
How do you decide?

Consider these explorations for the future:
- *Discovering the consequences for specific actions by individuals, groups, governments, including in businesses and the economy*
- *Discovering what counts and what matters vs. what is trivial, unimportant, wasteful, unjust*
- *Discovering the purpose and use of government*
  - *To do what the individual cannot do alone—all together for the common good, such as infrastructure, education, health care, environmental standards, defense*
  - *To protect the weak and helpless because the strong and wealthy have no trouble creating advantages*
  - *To provide equality and justice everywhere and for all*

- *Discovering justice and equity*
- *Discovering individual responsibility vs. group responsibility, when to act alone and when to act together*
- *Discovering right uses of power vs. wrong uses of power in the individual, group, and nation*
- *Discovering right uses of money vs. wrong uses of money*
- *Discovering economic sufficiency vs. scarcity [See Your Money or your Life by Joe Dominguez and Vicki Robin]*
  -What is enough?
  -When is enough?
  -What is excess?
  -What is selfish?
- *Discovering what creates human dignity*
- *Discovering what constitutes a stimulating and interesting life*
- *Discovering the difference between joy and fun*
- *Discovering the meaning of living an adventurous and responsible life*
- *Discovering the difference between risk and passivity, between courage and thrills*
- *Discovering economic fairness*
- *Discovering what our use of money shows about our values*

9.2.0 *Thought Experiment, continuing into the future: Freedom and Awareness in Creating a Self-Governing Society*

- *What are the characteristics of a society that is capable of self-governance?*
- *How can we create such a society?*
- *How can we build an individual sense of independence and freedom for both men and women?*
- *How can we build from the local level first, the ground up?*
- *How can we accept the processes of life and the chaos of Growth? (Decay is static, lifeless, and "controlled." Would we rather choose what is safe, smooth, and secure?)*

A Practical Handbook for Moral Growth

- *How can we avoid thoughtless rebellions that blindly tear down?*
- *How can we build up freedom at home and abroad by encouraging*
  Self-governance under equitable laws
  Gender equity
  Responsibility
  Will and fortitude
  Effort and work
  Struggle and willingness to endure frustration

9.3.0 *Thought Experiment, continuing into the future: Freedom and Awareness in Creating a Self-Governing Individual*

- *How can we become aware of our definitions and sources of true abundance— economically, psychologically, intellectually, physically, and spiritually?*
- *How can we become aware of our freedom to act, learn, love, and choose?*
- *How can we become aware of our need to be free from fear, threat, and injustice as well as the needs of others to be free from fear, threat, and injustice?*
- *How can we become aware of our freedom to be rational as opposed to irrational?*
- *How can we become aware of our freedom to be personally responsible and active as opposed to being passive and helpless?*
- *How can we learn to recognize the consequences of our individual choices?*
- *How can we learn the necessity of courage?*

10.0.0 Wisdom from Many Places, Traditions, and Voices: A Bibliography of some ideas influencing the text

David (ca. 1000 BCE; written ca. 3rd-5th century BCE):
Psalm 7:14-16: "Behold the wicked man conceives evil, / and is pregnant with mischief / and brings forth lies. / He makes a pit, digging it out, / and falls into the hole which he has made. / His mischief returns upon his own head, / and on his own pate his violence descends."
Psalm 34: 14: "Depart from evil, and do good; / seek peace, and pursue it."

Solomon (ca. 900 BCE; written ca. 3rd century BCE):
Proverbs 1: 19: "Such are the ways of all who get gain by violence; / it takes away the life of its possessors."

Micah (ca. 742-687 BCE):
Micah 6:8: "He has showed you, O man, what is good; and what does the Lord require of you but to do justice, and to love kindness, and to walk humbly with your God?"

Lao tse [Lao tzu] (b. 604 BCE), Tao te ching #17 (Trans. Stephen Mitchell):
"The Master doesn't talk, he acts. / When his work is done, / the people say, 'Amazing: / we did it all by ourselves.' "

Buddha [Siddhartha Gautama; Siddhatta Gotama] (b. 565 BCE), The Dhammapada (Trans. Acharya Buddharakkhita)
"It may be well with the evil-doer as long as the evil ripens not. But when it does ripen, then the evil-doer sees the painful results of his evil deeds." #119

A Practical Handbook for Moral Growth

"It may be ill with the doer of good as long as the good ripens not. But when it does ripen, then the doer of good sees the pleasant results of his good deeds." #120

"If on the hand there is no wound, one may carry even poison in it. Poison does not affect one who is free from wounds. For him who does no evil, there is no ill." #124

Confucius (551-479 BCE), The Great Digest:

"Wanting good government in their states, they first established order in their own families; wanting order in the home, they first disciplined themselves."

Aristotle (384-322 BCE):

Friendship is "the promotion of the other's good for the other's own sake."

Paul (d. ca. 64 AD)

Galatians 3: 28: "There is neither Jew nor Greek, there is neither slave nor free, there is neither male nor female; for you are all one in Christ Jesus." (ca. 49-58 AD)

Galatians 5: 22-23: "The Fruit of the Spirit is love, joy, peace, patience, kindness, goodness, faithfulness, gentleness, and self control." (ca. 49-58 AD)

II Corinthians 3:17: "Now the Lord is the Spirit, and where the Spirit of the Lord is, there is freedom." (ca. 57-90 AD)

Philippians 4: 8: "Finally, brethren, whatever is true, whatever is honorable, whatever is just, whatever is pure, whatever is lovely, whatever is gracious, if there is any excellence, if there is anything worthy of praise, think about these things." (ca 62 AD)

I Timothy 6: 10a: "For the love of money is the root of all evils."

Great Law of the Haudenosaunee [Iroquois], (ca. 1000-1450):
"In our every deliberation, we must consider the impact of our decisions on the next seven generations."

Rumi (1207-1273), Open Secret (Trans. John Moyne and Colman Barks):
"Let the beauty we love be what we do. / There are hundreds of ways to kneel and kiss the ground."

John Donne (1572-1631), "Meditation XVII from Devotions upon Emergent Occasions" (1623):
"No man is an island, entire of itself; every man is a piece of the continent, a part of the main. [. . .] Any man's death diminishes me, because I am involved in Mankind; and therefore never send to know for whom the bell tolls; it tolls for thee."

John Milton (1608-1674), Areopagitica (1644):
"For books are not absolutely dead things, but do contain a potency of life in them to be as active as that soul was whose progeny they are [. . . . W]ho kills a man kills a reasonable creature, God's image; but he who destroys a good book, kills reason itself, kills the image of God, as it were, in the eye [. . . .][,] the breath of reason   itself,   slays   an immortality rather than a life."
"I cannot praise a fugitive and cloistered virtue, unexercised and unbreathed, that never sallies out and sees her adversary, but slinks out of the race where that immortal garland is to be run for, not without dust and heat. [. . . T]hat which purifies us is trial, and trial is by what is contrary.   That virtue therefore which is but a youngling in the contemplation of evil, and knows not the utmost that vice promises to her followers, and rejects it, is but a blank virtue, not a pure; her whiteness is but an excremental [external] whiteness [. . .]."

A Practical Handbook for Moral Growth 138

"When God gave him [Adam] reason, he gave him freedom to choose, for reason is but choosing [. . . .] We ourselves esteem not of that obedience, or love, or gift, which is of force."

"Give me the liberty to know, to utter, and to argue freely according to conscience, above all liberties."

Blaise Pascal (1623-1662):

"Just because you cannot understand a thing, it does not cease to exist."

Declaration of Independence (July 4, 1776):

"We hold these truths to be self-evident, that all men are created equal, that they are endowed by their Creator with certain unalienable Rights, that among these are Life, Liberty, and the pursuit of Happiness. That to secure these rights, Governments are instituted among Men, deriving their just powers from the consent of the governed."

United States Constitution (September 17, 1787):

"We the people of the United States, in Order to form a more perfect Union, establish Justice, insure domestic Tranquility, provide for the common Defense, promote the general Welfare, and secure the Blessings of Liberty to ourselves and our Posterity, do ordain and establish this Constitution for the United States of America."

Bill of Rights (March 4, 1789):

"Congress shall make no law respecting an establishment of religion, or prohibiting the free exercise thereof; or abridging the freedom of speech, or of the press; or the right of the people peaceably to assemble, and to petition the Government for a redress of grievances."

Alexis de Tocqueville (1805-1859):

"Life is to be entered upon with courage."

John Stuart Mill (1806-1873):

"Those only are happy who have their minds fixed on some object other than their own happiness; on the happiness of others, on the improvement of mankind, even on some art or pursuit, followed not as a means, but as itself an ideal end. Aiming thus at something else, they find happiness by the way."

Abraham Lincoln (1809-1865), The Gettysburg Address (November 19, 1863):

"Four score and seven years ago our fathers brought forth on this continent a new nation, conceived in Liberty, and dedicated to the proposition that all men are created equal.

[. . . F]or us to be here dedicated to the great task remaining before us [. . .] that government of the people, by the people, for the people, shall not perish from the earth."

Oliver Wendell Holmes (1809-1894):

"Taxes are the price we pay for civilization."

Henry David Thoreau (1817-1862):

On the Duty of Civil Disobedience (speech 1848; 1849):

"It is truly enough said, that a corporation has no conscience; but a corporation of conscientious men is a corporation *with* a conscience."

"Why does [government] not encourage its citizens to be on the alert to point out its faults [. . .]? Why does it always crucify Christ, and excommunicate Copernicus and Luther, and pronounce Washington and Franklin rebels?"

Walden (1854):

"In the long run men hit only what they aim at. Therefore, though they should fail immediately, they had better aim at something high."

("Economy")

A Practical Handbook for Moral Growth

"The cost of a thing is the amount of what I will call life which is required to be exchanged for it, immediately or in the long run." ("Economy")

"No doubt another *may* also think for me; but it is not therefore desirable that he should do so to the exclusion of my thinking for myself." ("Economy")

"There are a thousand hacking at the branches of evil to one who is striking at the root, and it may be that he who bestows the largest amount of time and money on the needy is doing the most by his mode of life to produce that misery which he strives in vain to relieve." ("Economy")

" [. . . O]ur vision does not penetrate the surface of things. We think that that *is* which *appears* to be." ("What I Lived For)

"'You who govern public affairs, what need have you to employ punishments? Love virtue, and the people will be virtuous.'" ("The Bean Field")

"Our whole life is startlingly moral. There is never an instant's truce between virtue and vice. Goodness is the only investment that never fails." ("Higher Laws")

"A single gentle rain makes the grass many shades greener. So our prospects brighten on the influx of better thoughts." ("Spring")

"Say what you have to say, not what you ought. Any truth is better than make-believe." ("Conclusion")

"However mean your life is, meet it and live it; do not shun it and call it hard names. [. . .] It looks poorest when you are richest. The fault finder will find faults even in paradise. Love your life, poor as it is." ("Conclusion")

Chief Standing Bear (Ponca tribe, d. 1908):
"Lack of respect for growing, living things soon [leads] to lack of respect for humans too."

Emily Dickinson (1830-1886):
"To live is so startling it leaves little time for anything else."

Theodore Roosevelt (1858-1919): "Only those who are fit to live do not fear to die. And none are fit to die who have shrunk from the joy of life and the duty of life. Both life and death are parts of the same great adventure."

Frederick Jackson Turner (1861-1932), "The Significance of History," Collected Essays:
"Thoughts and feelings flow into deeds."

Mahatma Gandhi [Mohandas Karamchand Gandhi] (1869-1948):
"Live as if you were to die tomorrow. Learn as if you were to live forever."

Albert Schweitzer (1875-1965):
"Man has lost the capacity to foresee and forestall. He will end by destroying the earth."

Joseph Stalin (1878-1953):
"A single death is a tragedy; a million deaths is a statistic."

Albert Einstein (1879-1955), personal letter 1950:
"A human being is part of the whole, called by us 'Universe', a part limited in time and space. He experiences himself, his thoughts and feelings as something separated from the rest—a kind of optical delusion of his consciousness. This delusion is a kind of prison for us, restricting us to our personal desires and to affection for a few persons nearest to us. Our task is to free ourselves from this prison by widening our circle of compassion to embrace all living creatures and the whole of nature in its beauty."

Eleanor Roosevelt (1884-1962):

"Life must be lived and curiosity kept alive. One must never, for whatever reason, turn his back on life."

Aldo Leopold (1887-1948), <u>Sand County Almanac with Essays on Conservation from Round River</u> (1949):

"We grieve only for what we know." ("July")

"[. . . A]ll men, by what they think about and wish for, in effect wield all tools. [Philosophy] knows that men thus determine by their manner of thinking and wishing, whether it is worthwhile to wield any." ("Axe in Hand")

"Harmony with land is like harmony with a friend; you cannot cherish his right hand and chop off his left. That is to say, you cannot love game and hate predators; you cannot conserve the waters and waste the ranges; you cannot build the forest and mine the farm. The land is one organism." ("The Round River")

"An ethic, ecologically, is a limitation on freedom of action in the struggle for existence. An ethic, philosophically, is a differentiation of social from anti-social conduct. These are two definitions of one thing. The thing has its origin in the tendency of interdependent individuals or groups to evolve modes of co-operation [. . . .] in which the original free-for-all competition has been replaced, in part, by co-operative mechanisms with an ethical content." ("The Land Ethic: The Ethical Sequence")

"Individual thinkers since the days of Ezekiel and Isaiah have asserted that the despoliation of land is not only inexpedient but wrong. Society, however, has not yet affirmed their belief." ("The Land Ethic")

"All ethics so far evolved rest upon a single premise: that the individual is a member of a community of interdependent parts. [. . . .] The land ethic simply enlarges the boundaries of the community to include soils, waters, plants, and animals, or collectively: the land." ("The Land Ethic")

"In short, a land ethic changes the role of *Homo sapiens* from conqueror of the land-community to plain member and citizen of it. It implies respect for his fellow-members, and also respect for the community as such." ("The Land Ethic")

"No important change in ethics was ever accomplished without an internal change in our intellectual emphasis, loyalties, affections, and convictions. The proof that conservation has not yet touched these foundations of conduct lies in the fact that philosophy and religion have not heard of it. In our attempt to make conservation easy, we have made it trivial." ("The Land Ethic")

"We can be ethical only in relation to something we can see, feel, understand, love, or otherwise have faith in." ("The Land Ethic")

"A land ethic, then, reflects the existence of an ecological conscience, and this in turn reflects a conviction of individual responsibility for the health of the land. Health is the capacity of the land for self-renewal." ("The Land Ethic")

"The evolution of a land ethic is an intellectual as well as emotional process. [. . .] The mechanism of operation is the same for any ethic: social approbation for right actions: social disapproval for wrong actions. By and large, our present problem is one of attitudes and implements. We are remodeling the Alhambra with a steam-shovel, and we are proud of our yardage." ("The Land Ethic")

J.R.R.Tolkien (1892-1973), <u>The Lord of the Rings</u> (1948):
"Many that live deserve death. And some that die deserve life. Can you give it to them? Then be not too eager to deal out death in the name of justice, fearing for your own safety. Even the wise cannot see all ends."

Pastor Martin Niemoller (1892-1984):
"In Germany [the Nazis] came first for the Communists, and I didn't speak up because I wasn't a Communist. Then they came for the trade unionists, and I didn't speak up because I wasn't a trade unionist. Then

they came for the Jews, and I didn't speak up because I wasn't a Jew. Then they came for the Catholics, and I didn't speak up because I was a Protestant. Then they came for me, and by that time there was no one left to speak up."

E.F. Schumacher (1911-1977, <u>Small is Beautiful: Economics as if People Mattered</u> (1973):
"The smart person solves a problem. The genius avoids it."

Barry Commoner (b. 1917), <u>The Closing Circle: Nature, Man, and Technology</u> (1971):
"The natural tendency to think of only one thing at a time is the chief reason why we have failed to understand the environment and have blundered into destroying it."

John Fowles (1926-2005):
"What we see is not necessarily the whole truth any more than the tree we see above ground is the whole tree."

Edward Abbey (1927-1989), "Water," <u>Desert Solitaire</u> (1968):
"Where there is no joy there can be no courage; and without courage all other virtues are useless."

Eli Wiesel (b. 1928):
"The opposite of love is not hate, but indifference."

Christopher Lasch (1932-1994), <u>The Culture of Narcissism</u> (1979):
"Strictly speaking, however, modern advertising seeks to promote not so much self-indulgence as self-doubt. It seeks to create needs, not to fulfill them; to generate new anxieties instead of allaying old ones."

Woody Allen (b. 1935):
"80% of success is showing up."

Bob Dylan (b. 1941), "It's Airight, Ma (I'm Only Bleeding)" (1965):
"He not busy being born is busy dying."

Christopher Vecsey, American Indian Environments (1980):
"Ethics are limitations of freedom based on consideration for the welfare and feelings of others. They form a structure of morally proper action."

William McDonough (b. 1951) and **Michael Braungart**, Cradle to Cradle: Remaking the Way We Make Things (2002):
"Poor design [...] reaches far beyond our own life span. It perpetuates what we call *intergenerational remote tyranny*—our tyranny over future generations through the effects of our actions today." (43)
"Insanity has been defined as doing the same thing over and over and expecting a different outcome. Negligence is described as doing the same thing over and over even though you know it is dangerous, stupid, or wrong." (117)

Yoga saying (anonymous):
"The way you do anything is the way you do everything."

A Practical Handbook for Moral Growth 146

11.0.0 Using this Handbook

Living as Though There Is a Tomorrow, Creating the Future by Choice Using Reason, Duty, Love, and Belief: A Practical Handbook for Moral Growth outlines a practical and unified way of seeing the world and thinking about our places in it. It recommends some common public language concerning morality. It provides questions to consider. It asks what a humanitarian and environmental ethic would look like if we believe that our choices should tend toward moral Growth. You provide the answers and the analysis. You bring your personal observations and your skills and expertise.

No learning is permanent—as history and our own experience warn us. **Each generation must repeat the learning process for itself.** No person automatically inherits learning or personal ethics from another, even though we are each strongly influenced by those around us. **Exploring and discovering humanitarian and environmental ethics is a personal process that must be deliberately repeated in each individual if moral Growth is to continue.** If we choose ethical Growth, then we cannot afford to make the mistake of assuming that others know or understand what we have come to know and understand. We must each make the personal effort for ourselves.

Each of us fits into multiple places in the worlds of family, business, education, institutions, civil society, and government. You should feel free to add your own particular skills and knowledge. Base the discussions outlined here on your particular needs. What follows is a list of ideas of who can use this Practical Handbook, what you might use it for, and why and how you might use it. As an individual of conscience, you carry that conscience with you into the world wherever you go.

Living As Though There Is a Tomorrow

Who? individuals
families
small and large groups with common interests
private businesses of all sizes
investors
elected and appointed officials at every level of government
officials and workers in public and private offices
volunteers of all types
educators at all levels
classes studying critical thinking and ethics in all disciplines
social groups, office groups, educational groups
departments, agencies, schools, and universities
non-governmental and governmental organizations
religious and philosophical groups

What? Read the entire book, studying each section in turn.
Pick and choose which topics to focus on based on interest (read 1.0.0, 2.0.0., and 2.1.0 first).
Choose topics related directly to your specialty or work (read 1.0.0, 2.0.0, and 2.1.0 first).
Study the principle of moral Growth and apply it to processes in your field or discipline.
Analyze policies and procedures of your business, school, agency, etc. using the principles of Growth to create your own Thought Experiments.

Where? Anywhere

When? Anytime and repeatedly
Studies can be spread out over months, weeks, a few days, or a day or two focused meeting or conference.
Studies can and should be repeated based on new behaviors or actions or needs.

A Practical Handbook for Moral Growth   148

Studies can and should be repeated for new people in any group.

Studies can and should be repeated for those who have read and thought about these issues before—they will always have new insights and experiences to bring to the discussions.

Continued regular analysis of newly proposed policies, laws, and procedures based on principles of Growth can and should be a habit.

Why?   A democracy depends on ethical Growth in its citizens, its officials, its representative groups, its schools, its leaders and followers at all levels.

Growth increases mental, emotional, intellectual, spiritual, and physical health.

How?   Choose an issue or problem.

Assuming moral Growth is among your goals, identify the outcome(s) you want to aim for.

Analyze <u>both</u> what to do and why.

General process:

- Study the Prologue and the Model of Moral Growth and Decay (1.0.0, 2.0.0, 2.1.0)
- Mark the list of characteristics of moral Growth and moral Decay as a reference.
- Realize that not everyone will value moral Growth in a given situation and some will not value moral Growth at all.
- Discuss problems or issues to be understood and/or resolved in your area of special interest (small and large group discussions).
- In the case of large groups, use small groups to suggest the problems or issues for possible focused in-depth discussion.

- Choose common issues or interests by consensus or vote among the larger group.
- Ask questions about the specific problem and determine specific actions and behaviors to focus on (small and large group discussions):
- In this specific case,_____, if we want moral Growth as a whole—
  1. How can we increase attraction to or love of life and its natural processes, even if they sometimes are chaotic and we cannot have complete control?
  2. How can we decrease attraction to or love of death, violence, force, power, and mechanism?
  3. How can we encourage love of others in ourselves or those we influence?
  4. How can we encourage love of our neighbors?
  5. How can we encourage love of strangers, seeing them as fellow humans?
  6. How can we encourage love of nature, including both living and non-living nature (the land and everything on, under, and in it)?
  7. How can we decrease extreme self-love and self-focus?
  8. How can we decrease the need for absolute or unthinking obedience?
  9. How can we encourage actions based on reason and independence?
  10. How can we encourage actions based on personal and group freedom?
  11. How can we encourage responsibility and courage in personal choices?
  12. How can we discourage parasitic dependence?
  13. How can we reduce fears and threats?
  14. How can we reduce authoritarianism?

Discuss and examine your choices and their natural or logical consequences, including both positive and negative results by taking human nature and real-life knowledge into account. Honesty is valuable. Neither cynicism nor rose-colored glasses are useful. Design laws, rules, policies, procedures, behaviors, and actions for yourself and your group that will encourage moral Growth.

12.0.0 Appendix
Speech for the Oxford Round Table
Global Warming and Sustainable Development:
Governing a Crisis
Oxford Round Table, August 12-17, 2007
St. Anne's College, Oxford University, Oxford, England

Growth: A Foundation for Sustainable
Environmental and Humanitarian Ethics
By Phyllis Ballata

How did we get to where we are? How could this evil have happened? These are hard questions, but we can examine Erich Fromm's model of the Syndrome of Growth and the Syndrome of Decay, which he wrote as he struggled with the questions of World War II, and expand his concepts into a sustainable humanitarian and environmental ethic. This ethic can combine all the deep questions of life—both the human and the natural. We can foresee and forestall as Albert Schweitzer admonished us to do.

I have been haunted since I've been here in Oxford by the ghosts of writers asking to be heard. [. . . You have brought inspiring reports from the world of science and engineering, but] we need to hear the voices of the storyteller, the poet, and the philosopher.

As Toni Morrison (Nobel Literature Prize winner, black American, woman) and Tim O'Brien (white, male, Minnesota Vietnam veteran) agree: fiction tells the truth, not just the facts: "Facts can exist without human intelligence, but truth cannot" [Morrison, "Inventing the Truth"], and "Story-truth is truer sometimes than happening truth" [O'Brien, The Things They Carried].

In "Ozymandias" the poet Percy Bysshe Shelley speaks for a "traveler from an antique land." As he stands in the Egyptian desert looking at the fallen and broken statue of a great and powerful ruler, he sees that the artist-sculptor has not been blinded by the power and wealth of the king, for he has read the king's decayed heart and carved his judgment into the "wrinkled lip and sneer of cold command." The poet sees human pride and arrogance and fear: "'My name is Ozymandias, king of kings: / Look on my works, ye Mighty, and despair!' / Nothing beside remains. . . . The lone and level sands stretch far away."

This is the essence of the universal human characteristic that Fromm calls Decay. We all know it [and recognize it]. . . .

In order to live sustainably [on both humanitarian and environmental levels], we have to choose to live as though there is a tomorrow. This moral Growth is required of us as individuals, in our families, in our work, in our institutions, and in our governments.

These are the definitions—the attributes—that make up the Syndrome of Decay and the Syndrome of Growth:
The Syndrome of Decay is characterized by
- attraction to or love of death, violence, and mechanism,
- extreme self-love,
- dependence and fear.

The Syndrome of Growth is characterized by
- attraction to or love of life,
- love of others that moves out from the self to neighbors, strangers, and nature or all living things (even, as Aldo Leopold would argue, to the land itself, the air, and the waters),
- willingness to risk the responsibility of independence, freedom, and choice.

Based on these characteristics, we might assume that surely everyone would choose Growth. Not true.

Decay in everyday life at all levels is eminently practical and rational. We look out for #1. We find ways to achieve immediate personal or select group advantage and power. We believe that what we see momentarily as a worthy goal justifies any means.

Growth, on the other hand, often appears irrational and impractical because the good of the greater community often comes before personal interests. Long term consequences influence our choices. This is living as though there is a tomorrow, but we may not gain immediate personal payback or advantage.

We all choose Decay sometimes in order to win the advantage for ourselves or for our group: in the family, at work, in the voting booth, and in international affairs. Machiavelli's advice to the Prince is entirely logical and practical. To maintain and enlarge power and wealth, he must choose Decay. He may pretend to believe in the attributes of Growth, but he must never weaken himself by acting on them.

Let's look at some current examples:

In the protection of New Orleans, we chose to tightly constrict the river with levees and allow no "worthless" floodplains; we chose to create shipping channels that tore up the swamps and marshes; we chose to cut down the forests and cypress groves for immediate gain; we chose to dismantle the vegetation on barrier islands for the sake of expensive housing and recreation; and we chose to build many city neighborhoods well below sea level. Why? Because we truly believed in the power and invincibility of our machines, in the demands of our wealth producing processes, and in our ability to outsmart and conquer

A Practical Handbook for Moral Growth 154

nature. The natural protections were destroyed. We had no respect, thought, or imagination for the systems that actually worked. We didn't want to know why they worked or how we could cooperate with them. Our answer was short term, violent, dependent on machines, and centered only on our immediate desires to create wealth and power—leaving us vulnerable and helpless in the end.

We create cities filled with green lawns, golf courses, and swimming pools in the desert. We pump antique water out of aquifers to flush a million toilets and to spray into the air for coordinated light and music shows. We race over the fragile soils, tearing up the ground and muddying the few water holes for "fun." Our hotels rise into the sky, but we never think to wonder what happened to the gorgeous hanging gardens of Babylon.

We want cheap fish, so we vacuum everything out of the sea, throwing back the "worthless" dead by-catch and keeping the quarterly profit to pay the executives, the shareholders, and the loans for even more enormous factory ships to win the competition to suck out the last fish. Meanwhile, we fight against marine reserves that might help replenish a little of the legendary richness of the sea by providing small sanctuaries for future reproduction because they prevent complete harvesting of resources today.

We want cheap oil for our petroleum culture, so we wage wars. We want cheap energy, so we subsidize nuclear power plants with waste that will be toxic for at least as long into the future as the time back to the last ice age, longer than human civilizations have so far existed, if it isn't made into nuclear weapons first. We reward centralized, highly vulnerable systems in every way politically possible. We don't want a village windmill or solar cells on every roof top or a manure digester in every farmyard or garbage-dump methane to create our energy. And we certainly don't want efficient transportation—because it is not profitable enough today.

We want cheap chicken, beef, and pork, so we create factory farms and drive the integrated, sustainable farmer out of business. Special subsidies are handed out to corporate investors; special rules allow lakes of manure and acres of animals packed together; special corporate protections prevent consumers from knowing where their meat comes from, whether the workers were paid a fair wage and worked in safe conditions, or whether they are eating growth hormones and antibiotics.

These examples show Decay at work—living as though there is no tomorrow—using control and force to achieve "my" interests, "my" gain, "my" power in "my" lifetime and in "my" bank account—yet at the same time driven by fear and extreme dependence on our ownership of material things and our imagined power over nature.

"'Look on my works, ye Mighty, and despair'"—despair of ever matching my power and my wealth.

"Fool, this night your soul will be required of you."

"'Look on my works, ye Mighty, and despair'"—despair because of the power and wealth and "sneer of cold command" nothing remains. "The lone and level sands stretch far away."

Growth is hard. Decay is easy, practical, and effective—temporarily. But with Decay, there is no tomorrow.

Aldo Leopold in "The Land Ethic" says, "No important change in ethics was ever accomplished without an internal change in our intellectual emphasis, loyalties, affections, and convictions." We

A Practical Handbook for Moral Growth 156

must deal with the whole of Growth: our <u>reason</u>, our sense of <u>duty</u>, our <u>love</u>, our <u>belief</u>. **All** must be present inside of each of us in order to accomplish a change in ethics toward Growth, rather than Decay.

The ghost of J.R.R. Tolkien writing here at Oxford has been hovering over us this week. Tolkien's story of struggle and temptation in <u>The Lord of the Rings</u> has been speaking of the heart of love, courage, life, and sacrifice opposing the heart of iron, death, hate, and violent power. His themes and characters are speaking to us.

Listen:

- In the darkest hour, Legolas says to Aragorn: I was wrong to despair. Forgive me.

- There is always hope.

- Even the littlest among us has the power to make a difference.

ISBN 142517290-3

9 781425 172909